CENSUS OF INDIA 1931

Census of India 1871-1951, 9 Sets In 384 Bindings (9788121258876) Rs. 700000

Census of India 1931, 28 Vols. In 52 Bindings (9788121271233) Rs. 102000

1. India - Report (9788121276153) Rs. 2820 (Vol. I, Pt. 1)
2. India - Imperial Tables (9788121276139) Rs. 3210 (Vol. I, Pt. 2)
3. India - Ethnographical and Administration Report (9788121276115) Rs. 2900 (Vol. I, Pt. 3 & 5)
4. The Andaman And Nicobar Islands - Report, Tables (9788121276078) Rs. 720 (Vol. II, Pt. 1, Pt. 2)
5. Assam - Report (9788121276054) Rs. 1340 (Vol. III, Pt. 1)
6. Assam - Tables and Administrative Report (9788121276030) Rs. 1830 (Vol. III, Pt. 2 & 3)
7. Baluchistan - Report, Imeprial and Provincial Tables and Administrative Report (9788121276016) Rs. 2320 (Vol. IV, Pt. 1 & 2 & 3)
8. Bengal & Sikkim - Report (9788121275972) Rs. 2860 (Vol. V, Pt. 1)
9. Bengal & Sikkim - Tables (9788121275958) Rs. 1660 (Vol. V, Pt. 2)
10. Calcutta (9788121275910) Rs. 960 (Vol. VI, Pt. 1 & 2)
11. Bengal, Sikkim And Calcutta - Administrative Report (9788121275934) Rs. 580 (Vol. V & VI, Pt. 3)
12. Bihar And Orissa - Report (9788121275897) Rs. 1780 (Vol. VII, Pt. 1)
13. Bihar And Orissa - Tables and Administrative Report (9788121275873) Rs. 1190 (Vol. VII, Pt. 2 & 3)
14. Bombay Presidency - General Report (9788121275835) Rs. 3620 (Vol. VIII, Pt. 1)
15. Bombay - Statistical tables (9788121275811) Rs. 3060 (Vol. VIII, Pt. 2)
16. Bombay Presidency Aden - report and tables and Administrative report (9788121275798) Rs. 520 (Vol. VIII, Pt. 3 & 4)
17. Cities of the Bombay Presidency Report & Statistical tables (9788121275750) Rs. 2020 (Vol. IX, Pt. 1 & 2)
18. The Western India States Agency, In Two Parts - The Report & The Statistical Tables (9788121275736) Rs. 2560 (Vol. X, Pt. 1 & 2)
19. Burma - Report (9788121275712) Rs. 1860 (Vol. XI, Pt. 1)
20. Burma - Tables and Administrative Report (9788121275699) Rs. 1690 (Vol. XI, Pt. 2 & 3)
21. Central Provinces & Berar - Report (9788121275651) Rs. 2340 (Vol. XII, Pt. 1)
22. Central Provinces & Berar - Tables and Administrative Report (9788121275637) Rs. 3120 (Vol. XII, Pt. 2 & 3)
23. Coorg - Report And Tables and Madras - Report (9788121275613) Rs. 2680 (Vol. XIV, Pt. 1)
24. Madras - Imperial And Provincial Tables and The Administration Report (9788121275576) Rs. 1950 (Vol. XIV, Pt. 2 & 4)
25. North - West Frontier Province - Report & Tables (9788121275538) Rs. 2300 (Vol. XV, Pt. 1 & 2)
26. Delhi - Report & Tables (9788121275514) Rs. 1180 (Vol. XVI, Pt. 1 & 2)
27. Punjab - Report (9788121275491) Rs. 2070 (Vol. XVII, Pt. 1)
28. Punjab - Tables (9788121275477) Rs. 1690 (Vol. XVII, Pt. 2)
29. United Provinces of Agra And Oudh - Report (9788121275453) Rs. 3380 (Vol. XVIII, Pt. 1)
30. United Provinces of Agra And Oudh - Imperial And Provincial Tables and Administrative (9788121275439) Rs. 3600 (Vol. XVIII, Pt. 2 & 3)
31. Baroda - Report (9788121275415) Rs. 2800 (Vol. XIX, Pt. 1)
32. Baroda - Tables (9788121275392) Rs. 730 (Vol. XIX, Pt. 2)
33. Baroda - Administrative (9788121275378) Rs. 780 (Vol. XIX, Pt. 3)
34. Central India Agency - Report (9788121275354) Rs. 1690 (Vol. XX, Pt. 1)
35. Central India Agency - Tables and Administrative Volume (9788121275330) Rs. 2260 (Vol. XX, Pt. 2 & 3)
36. Cochin - Report & Tables (9788121275293) Rs. 2460 (Vol. XXI, Pt. 1 & 2 - A & B.)
37. Gwalior - Report (9788121275279) Rs. 1470 (Vol. XXII, Pt. 1)
38. Gwalior - Tables (9788121275255) Rs. 980 (Vol. XXII, Pt. 2)
39. H. E. H. The Nizam's Dominions (Hyderabad State) - Report (9788121275231) Rs. 1540 (Vol. XXIII, Pt. 1)
40. H. E. H. The Nizam's Dominions (Hyderabad State) - Tables (9788121275217) Rs. 1510 (Vol. XXIII, Pt. 2)
41. Jammu & Kashmir State - Report (9788121275194) Rs. 2060 (Vol. XXIV, Pt. 1)
42. Jammu & Kashmir State - Imperial & State Tables (9788121275170) Rs. 1940 (Vol. XXIV, Pt. 2 & 3)
43. Mysore - Report (9788121275156) Rs. 1950 (Vol. XXV, Pt. 1)
44. Mysore - Tables (9788121275132) Rs. 1380 (Vol. XXV, Pt. 2)
45. Ajmer-Merwara - Report And Tables (9788121275118) Rs. 780 (Vol. XXVI)
46. Rajputana Agency And Ajmer-Merwara - Report and Tables and Administrative (9788121275095) Rs. 2380 (Vol. XXVII, Pt. 1 & 2)
47. Travancore - Report (9788121276092) Rs. 2960 (Vol. XXVIII, Pt. 1)
48. Travancore - Tables & Administrative (9788121275996) Rs. 1360 (Vol. XXVIII, Pt. 2 & 4)
49. Jaipur State- Report (9788121275859) Rs. 1280 (Pt. 1)
50. Jaipur State- Tables (9788121275774) Rs. 2030 (Pt. 2)
51. Mayurbhanj state- Report (9788121275675) Rs. 3180 (Pt. 1)
52. Mayurbhanj state- Tables (9788121275552) Rs. 3070 (Pt. 2)

Owing to the antiquity and rarity of this book, certain pages are regrettably absent, and readability is compromised due to the blurring of the original text. If you possess any insights regarding the availability of these missing sections, kindly inform us. Your assistance is crucial in ensuring the completion of this significant work for the benefit of future generations.

CENSUS OF INDIA, 1931

BOOK - 23: VOLUME - XIII

COORG

PART I - REPORT AND TABLES

VOLUME - XIV

MADRAS

PART I - REPORT

M. S. MANDANNA
&
M. W. M. YEATTS

GYAN

Published by

Gyan Publishing House
5, Ansari Road
Daryaganj, New Delhi-110002
Phone: 011-47034999, 9811692060
E-mail: books@gyanbooks.com

Distribution Network
gyanbooks.com
India, USA, Canada, UK, Australia

ISBN: 978-81-212-7123-3 (Set) 28 Vols. In 52 Bindings

ISBN: 978-81-212-7561-3 (PB) Vol. XIII, Pt. I & Vol. XIV, Pt. I

First Published, 1932

2nd Impression 2024

Printed at: Gyan Press, Delhi.

CENSUS OF INDIA 1931

CENSUS OF INDIA, 1931

VOLUME XIII

COORG

REPORT AND TABLES

BY

M. S. MANDANNA,

Deputy Director of Land Records and Agriculture, Coorg

MADRAS

PRINTED BY THE SUPERINTENDENT, GOVERNMENT PRESS, AND PUBLISHED BY THE GOVERNMENT OF INDIA CENTRAL PUBLICATION BRANCH, CALCUTTA

1932

CONTENTS

IMPERIAL SERIES—VOLUME XIII.

THE REPORT.

IMPERIAL TABLES.

PROVINCIAL TABLES.

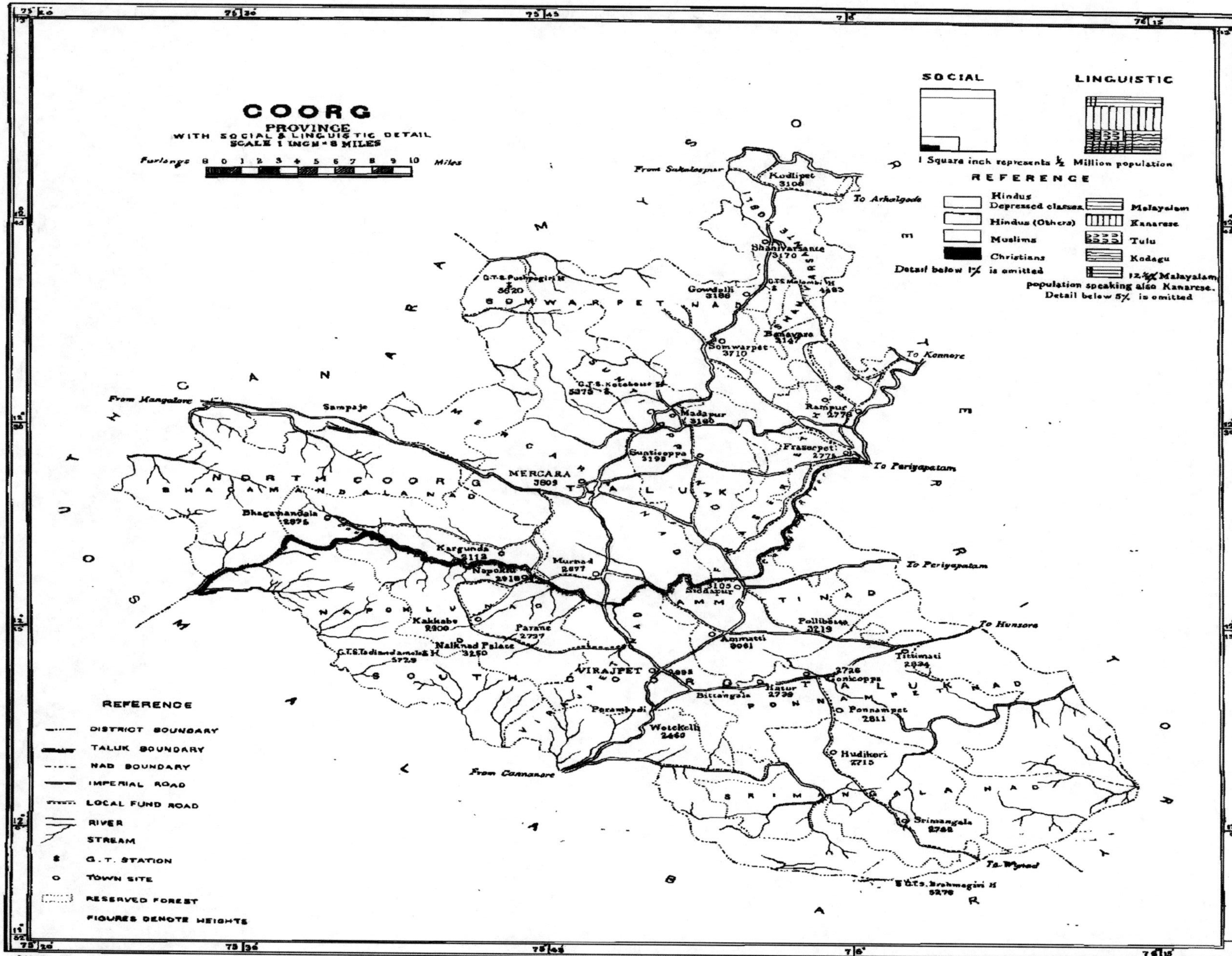

Reg. No. 70
Copies, 450

Prepared by
12-6-32
Draftsman

Helio Zinco Survey Office, Madras.
1932.
20. 6. 32
Deputy Director,
Land Records & Agriculture,
Coorg

CENSUS OF INDIA, 1931
COORG

IMPERIAL SERIES, VOLUME XIII

THE REPORT AND TABLES

INTRODUCTION.

THE Province of Coorg is a picturesque highland occupying the summits and the eastern and western slopes of the Western Ghats, clothed with primeval forests or grassy glades and broken by but few cultivated valleys. It is bounded on the west by South Kanara, on the south-west and south by Malabar and on the north and east by the Mysore State. The lofty barrier range of the Western Ghats, forms the continuous western frontier, with its highest peaks the Thadiandamole 5,729 feet and the Pushpagiri 5,620 feet above the sea. The main drainage of the country is towards the east. The largest river is the Kaveri, which, with its principal tributaries, the Hemavati, Laksmanathirtha, Kakkabe and Suvarnavati, flows in the easterly direction and strikes the Mysore frontier near Sirangala. The Barapolae is the only river worthy of name, which flows westward and passes into the district of Malabar.

2. The general supervision of the census operations in Coorg was, according to the practice followed since 1891, entrusted to the Census Superintendent of Madras. But, the report for the second time was written by a local officer, the statistics having been tabulated in Mangalore, which is one of the abstraction offices of the Madras Presidency. The suggestion to set up an abstraction office in Coorg was abandoned on account of the prohibitive cost. It is a matter for regret that even the proposal to depute a few clerks from this Province to help the abstraction office did not materialise with the result that it has not been found possible either to reconcile some discrepancies in figures or to offer reasonable explanations on these points. For example, it is seen in Imperial Table VIII, that there are 7 married persons among Coorgs and 2 among Gaudas, below the age of 6 years, though marriages at such an early age are absolutely unknown among these communities. The lack of information in such individual cases comes in the way of verification of the facts. It is not possible to offer any explanation for the reduction by nearly one-half in the Lingayet population. In spite of the special precautions taken during enumeration to exclude Jama Coorgs, who are not Coorgs by race, but are Vokkaligas holding land on Jama tenure, it is seen that some Jama Coorgs—Vokkaligas—have been shown as Coorgs this time also ; this has resulted in a somewhat inaccurate estimation of the population of Coorgs. Anyhow, this year's figures may be said to denote fairly accurately the population of the Coorgs. Again, while the actual Yerava population has been shown as 12,810, the number of persons returned as speaking the Yerava language is 10,026, and it is extremely difficult to offer any satisfactory explanation for this discrepancy. To ensure the correctness of the statistics and to facilitate the reconciliation of discrepancies, I commend once again the suggestion to depute at least one intelligent clerk from Coorg to the abstraction office in future. If the clerk sent to the abstraction office is subsequently employed to assist the officer entrusted with the work of writing the report, such difficulties as are pointed out above would, to an appreciable extent, be minimised. It is also desirable that the enumeration schedules should be sent back to Coorg to facilitate reference when the report is being written.

3. Turning to census operations proper, there were no substantial changes in the methods followed. The whole of Coorg excluding the two municipalities, had been divided into five separate charges for purposes of census operations in 1921, each taluk forming a separate charge. Consequent on the reduction of taluks into two during the decade, there were only two charges this time—the South Coorg and the North Coorg—the concerned Subedars being appointed as charge Superintendents thereof. The municipalities of Mercara and Virajpet formed two separate charges as before, the respective Presidents acting as charge Superintendents. There were in all 113 circles and 1,417 blocks against 127 circles and 1,431 blocks in 1921.

4. The house list having been prepared before August 1930, the house numbering was commenced in October and finished by the 15th November 1930. The preliminary enumeration was started on the 5th January in rural areas and on the 19th January 1931 in urban areas and completed by the end of the month. The rough schedules were thoroughly checked afterwards by the supervising staff and the corrected entries copied into the fair schedules. The final census took place on the 26th February 1931. The totals for each charge were received by the 28th February at Mercara and on the same day the district totals were telegraphed to the Census Commissioner with the Government of India and the Superintendent of Census Operations, Madras. In 1921 these totals were telegraphed only on the fourth day after the census. The difference between the provincial and the actual totals was 238 against 621 in 1921, the actual figures preponderating. The enumeration of the forest tribes was also conducted on the night of the final census day without difficulty with the co-operation of the Forest Department.

5. In spite of the attempts of a few misguided youths in South Coorg to start a non-co-operation campaign in regard to census work, which was promptly put down, the public at large rendered honorary services most ungrudgingly and this, in no small measure, contributed to the success of the census operations.

6. Rao Bahadur K. Chengappa, B. A., Assistant Commissioner and District Magistrate of Coorg, under whose guidance and supervision the report is written, was throughout in charge of the census operations. I am very much indebted to him for the valuable assistance rendered to me in writing the report.

CHAPTER I.

DISTRIBUTION AND MOVEMENT OF POPULATION.

Changes in area.

THE area of the province is 1,593 square miles and shows an increase of 11 square miles over the figure noted in the last census report. There has been no change in the boundary of the province and the difference in area is due to the increase that is found in South Coorg through computation from the latest surveys. The information relating to the revised area of the province was received from the Surveyor-General of India long after the tables, both imperial and provincial, were printed and it is, therefore, not possible for the purposes of this census to take into account this corrected area. It is, however, necessary to point out that the density figures can only be taken as correct subject to the discrepancy now discovered to exist between the area of the province now furnished by the Surveyor-General and the area hitherto accepted as authoritative. An explanatory note to clear this point is put up below Imperial Table I. The outer boundary did not undergo any alteration, but there were several redistributions of taluks and villages during the decade. The five taluks in existence prior to 1921 were for administrative purposes reduced to four in 1921, to three in 1922 and finally to two in 1923, which are now designated as North Coorg and South Coorg taluks, the river Kaveri forming the dividing line. Of the five taluks in existence prior to 1921, Mercara, Nanjarajapatna and portions of Padinalknad and Yedenalknad taluks now form the North Coorg taluk, while the remaining portions of Padinalknad and Yedenalknad taluks and the whole of Kiggatnad taluk form the South Coorg taluk. Simultaneously with the reduction of the taluks to two, several villages were amalgamated for administrative reasons, bringing down the total number of villages from 378 to 298. For census purposes, however, the original villages are retained. The variation in the area and population of taluks is given below :—

At the census of 1921.						At the census of 1931.		
Taluk.	Area in square miles.	Population.	Taluks after re-adjustment of boundaries in 1923.	Area in square miles.	Population.	Taluks.	Area in square miles.	Population.
Kiggatnad ..	421	40,548	South Coorg	822	87,299	South Coorg	822	84,580
Padinalknad ..	395	29,236						
Yedenalknad ..	221	36,240						
Mercara	310	26,376	North Coorg	760	76,589	Norh Coorg	760	78,747
Nanjarajapatna ..	235	31,438						
Total ..	1,582	163,838		1,582	163,838		1,582	163,327

Meaning of population.

2. For statistical purposes two kinds of population are taken into account, viz., the *de jure* population and the *de facto* population. By *de jure* population is meant those persons who are normally resident in any locality, including those temporarily absent and excluding those temporarily present ; while *de facto* population means those persons who are found actually present in the locality at a particular part of time. The Indian Census being a *de facto* census, the term 'population' as employed in Coorg census represents the persons recorded as actually present at the final enumeration on the census night, i.e., 26th February 1931.

Summary of statistics.

3. The total number of persons enumerated on the census night was 163,327 as compared to 163,838 in 1921, which means a decrease of 511 persons. Taking the taluk population into consideration, there was an increase of 2,208 persons in North Coorg and a decrease of 2,719 persons in South Coorg. The increase of 4,781 in the number of persons born outside Coorg and enumerated within the Province, which is represented mostly by the immigrant population, coupled with the decrease of 511 in the total population, shows that the natural population has suffered a diminution in number. This is further borne out by the figures furnished in the vital statistics, which show an excess of 13,956 deaths over births during the decade. The increase in the immigrant population is more apparent than real. Most of the immigrant labourers working in the plantations return to their native place about the beginning of March soon

after they finish their work in the estates in which they are employed. The last census was taken on the 18th March 1921, when a considerable number of labourers must have left for their native land and the present census was taken on the 26th February when very few of the labourers had left the estates. It may be said that the increasing prosperity of the coffee industry in North Coorg and its decline in South Coorg accounts for the small increase in population in the former taluk and decrease in the latter taluk. The enumeration was, on the whole, conducted very satisfactorily and there is no reason to doubt its accuracy.

Density and variations. 4. The density of population in 1931 is 103 per square mile against 104 in 1921; there is hardly any difference in density in the two taluks. Subsidiary Table I gives the mean density for total and cultivated areas separately as also the normal rainfall and percentage of gross cultivated area under some of the principal crops of the Province. The only districts in Madras and Hyderabad, which have equal or lower density per square mile are Adilabad in Hyderabad, and Ganjam, Vizagapatam and Godavari Agencies and Sandur State in Madras Presidency. It is necessary to point out here that the density would rise to 154, if from the total area of 1,582 square miles (according to the Imperial Table), an area of 519 square miles of Reserve Forest is excluded.

Condition of the decade. 5. Coorg, as other parts of India, is pre-eminently agricultural and rice, the staple food of the province, is the main cultivation of the people. The only flourishing industry is coffee, cardamom being cultivated on a fairly large scale in the Western Ghats. Rubber, tea and agave are also cultivated in some parts of the province to a limited extent. All these cultivations except tea are being abandoned owing to their unproductivity. The season during the decade was normally favourable for both rice and coffee, except during 1924, when owing to an unusually heavy monsoon followed by unprecedented floods the crops suffered badly. The steady prices which ruled the markets for rice, which is the staple product, till 1929, enabled the ryots to tide over the difficulties occasioned by the seasonal vicissitudes, in spite of the increased cost of living. The sudden fall in the prices of food-stuffs from 1930, owing to general economic and trade depression, reduced the ryots to a miserable condition and damped their enthusiasm even for rice cultivation. The result was that the area under rice which was 84,587 acres in 1921 went down to 82,822 in 1931.

Public health. 6. At no time during the decade was scarcity for food experienced and there was no fear of any famine. The mortality in recent years shows signs of decrease and this may partly be attributed to the anti-malarial measures undertaken by the Government. There has been a steady decrease in birth-rate and the abnormal number of deaths among persons aged (both males and females) between 20 and 40 affords a plausible explanation for the decrease in the birth-rate.

Vital statistics. 7. There has been no change in the system of recording vital statistics. As usual, it was recorded in the nad offices in rural areas and by the two Municipalities in the urban areas. The excess of deaths over births by 13,956, according to Subsidiary Table *iii*, is not encouraging. It is difficult to gauge the exact incidence of births and deaths, among the natural and immigrant population separately. But there is reason to suppose that the excess of deaths over births, was more among the indigenous population, in view of the fact that there was a decrease of about 5,000 in the number of persons born and enumerated in Coorg. Birth control by artificial means is unknown to the average people and is rarely being practised even among the educated classes. On the other hand, the desire of the average individual appears to be to have as many children as is possible, irrespective of his economic position.

Movement of the population. 8. The movement of the natural population, except a few who go out for purposes of education and appointment, is negligible, since the people being mainly agriculturists, are closely bound to their own lands. The little movement that exists within the province is mainly among the immigrant population whose influx is to a very large extent influenced by the fluctuations of the coffee industry.

Occupied houses.

9. Imperial Table I shows the number of occupied houses for the whole of Coorg, and Provincial Table I gives similar information for the two taluks separately. The term 'house' means every dwelling with a separate main entrance of a normal and recognizable type and regularly used by persons entering the dwelling from the street or yard. The total number of houses recorded in 1931 was 33,906 against 31,399 in 1921. In the two towns of Mercara and Virajpet, the total population was 9,827 and occupied houses 1,947, against 8,841 and 1,753 respectively in 1921. In other words, there was an increase of 11·15 per cent in population and an increase of 11·06 per cent in the number of occupied houses. In the rural areas, the number of occupied houses showed an increase of 7 per cent and population a decrease of 1 per cent. The irresistible inference is that the Coorg joint family system is gradually breaking up owing to the growing tendency on the part of the newly married youths to detach themselves from the main ('Ayne') family and to live in separate houses near by. This is further substantiated by the fact that while according to Subsidiary Table *iv*, there has been a gradual increase in the number of houses per square mile since 1881, there has been a corresponding decrease in the number of persons per house since 1881.

Pressure of population.

10. The pressure of population on the means of subsistence does not show any considerable variation during the decade. On the other hand, the output of the staple food-stuffs continued to be much in excess of the local requirements with the result that the surplus paddy had to be disposed of during the past 3 years, even at ridiculously low prices.

i.—Density, Water-supply and Crops.

Province.	Mean density per square mile. — Of total area.	Mean density per square mile. — Of cultivated area.	Percentage of total area. — Cultivable.	Percentage of total area. — Net cultivated.	Percentage of cultivable area. — Net cultivated.	Percentage of cultivable area. — Double cropped.	Percentage of gross cultivated area which is irrigated.	Normal rainfall in inches.	Percentage of gross cultivated area under — Coffee.	Rice.	Ragi.	Other food crops.	Other crops.
1	2	3	4	5	6	7	8	9	10	11	12	13	14
Coorg	103·2	757·3	31·7	13·6	43·0	0·4	2·7	127·0	29·0	59·9	2·6	1·0	7·5

ii.—Area, Population, etc., of Taluks classified according to density.

Taluks with a population per square mile.	Number.	Area. — Actual.	Area. — Percentage to total.	Population. — Actual.	Population. — Percentage to total.	Variation since 1921. — Actual.	Variation since 1921. — Percentage.
1	2	3	4	5	6	7	8
Total ..	**2**	**1,582**	**100**	**163,327**	**100**	**— 511**	**— 0·3**
Under 100 ..	..	..	..	..	..	..	..
100–150	2	1,582	100	163,327	100	— 511	— 0·3
150–200 ..	..	..	..	..	..	..	..

iii.—Comparison with vital statistics.

Province.	In 1921–1930. Total number of — Births.	In 1921–1930. Total number of — Deaths.	Number per cent of population of 1921 of — Births.	Number per cent of population of 1921 of — Deaths.	Excess (+) or deficiency (—) of births over deaths.	Increase (+) or decrease (—) of population of 1931 compared with 1921.
1	2	3	4	5	6	7
Coorg	36,818	50,774	22·5	31·0	— 13,956	— 511

iv.—House-room, Density and Variation.

Year.	Houses. — Average number of houses per square mile.	Houses. — Average number of persons per house.	Mean density per square mile.	Variation in population. — Period.	Variation in population. — Percentage.
1	2	3	4	5	6
1881	14	8	113	1881–1891	— 2·9
1891	17	6	109	1891–1901	+ 4·4
1901	19	6	114	1901–1911	+ 3·1
1911	21	5	111	1911–1921	— 6·4
1921	20	5	103	1921–1931	— 0·3
1931	21	5	103	1881–1931	— 8·4

CHAPTER II.

POPULATION OF CITIES, TOWNS AND VILLAGES.

Reference to statistics.

THE statistics relating to population in urban and rural areas are given in Imperial Tables I to V and Provincial Table III. The three subsidiary tables appended at the end of this chapter show

(i) the distribution of the population between towns and villages,
(ii) the number per mille of total population and of each main religion who live in towns, and
(iii) the towns classified by population.

Population of towns.

2. Mercara and Virajpet are the only two towns in Coorg with a population of 5,995 and 3,832 respectively. For the purposes of census, a 'town' is defined to include all municipalities, civil lines, cantonments and every other continuous collection of houses inhabited by not less than 5,000 persons. Though Virajpet has a population of less than 5,000 persons it is considered as a town, on account of its importance as a principal trading centre and as a municipality possessing all the urban characteristics. The population in both these towns, which was gradually declining from 1881, showed for the first time an increase from 5,675 to 5,995 in Mercara and from 3,166 to 3,832 in Virajpet in 1931. The increase in Mercara consists of 114 males and 206 females and may partly be attributed to the influx of persons owing to the trading facilities provided by motor bus services and partly to the increase from 156 to 275 girls in the aided Girls High School, Mercara, during the decade. The increase of 454 males and 212 females in Virajpet, which represents 21 per cent of the population, is noticeable. The develpoment of the town into a prominent trading centre and the growing tendency of a considerable number of people in rural areas to take up residence in the town with their families account for this growth of population. Considering the religions, the only noticeable gain was among the Hindus in Virajpet to the extent of 605 persons or 39 per cent. The one Parsi family which was out of Coorg in 1921, was enumerated this time with the result that there were 27 of them in Mercara and Virajpet.

Village population.

3. A village in Coorg is not a residential but an administrative unit comprising several residential units or hamlets. The number of such villages was further reduced for administrative purposes from 378 to 298 by clubbing many villages during the decade. The number of villages having a population of 1,000 to 2,000 has increased from 18 to 20. Devanur, Chennayanakote, Kutta and Nokya in South Coorg, and Uluguli, Attur-Nallur and Kirgandur in North Coorg, which were classed as villages having a population of 500 to 1,000 in 1921, have now come to the category of villages having a population of 1,000 to 2,000 while the reverse is the case with Arameri, Karadigodu, Heggala, Kedamullur, Maithadi and Puliyeri villages in South Coorg. Villages with a population of 500 to 1,000 show an increase from 84 to 89. A general feature is that the village population is slightly decreasing in South Coorg and steadily increasing in North Coorg.

4. The average population per village is 406 as compared to 411 in 1921. While the total population of the province has gone down by 511, the urban population recorded a gain of 986. The village population, therefore, suffered a diminution of 1,497 persons. Further, a village by name Doddakanagala, which was perhaps temporarily uninhabited in 1921, was omitted in the village statement and consequently the number of villages has increased by one. This explains the decrease in population per village.

Distribution of population between towns and villages.

5. The number per mille of population residing in towns is 60, and in villages 940, as compared with 54 and 946 respectively in 1921. Except the educated classes in Government service and a few businessmen, others in general, still prefer their residence in villages on account of their close attachment to their privileged ancestral lands.

i.—Distribution of the Population between towns and villages.

Province.	Average population per		Number per mille residing in		Number per mille of urban population residing in towns with a population of		Number per mille of rural population residing in villages with a population of		
	Town.	Village.	Towns.	Villages.	5,000 to 10,000.	Under 5,000.	1,000 to 2,000.	500 to 1,000.	Under 500.
1	2	3	4	5	6	7	8	9	10
Coorg	4,914	406	60	940	610	390	172	390	438

ii.—Number per mille of total population and of each main religion who live in towns.

Province.	Number per mille who live in towns.				
	Total population.	Hindu.	Muslim.	Christian.	Jain.
1	2	3	4	5	6
Coorg	60	44	178	248	602

iii.—Towns classified by population.

Class.	Number of towns of each class in 1931.	Proportion to total urban population.	Females per 1,000 males.	Variation per cent in the population of towns as classed at previous censuses.					
				1921 to 1931.	1911 to 1921.	1901 to 1911.	1891 to 1901.	1881 to 1891.	1881 to 1931.
1	2	3	4	5	6	7	8	9	10
Total ..	***2***	***100***	***680***	***+ 11·2***	***− 11·4***	***− 9·4***	***− 4·1***	***− 11·4***	***− 24·2***
5,000 to 10,000.	1	61·0	749	+ 5·6	− 9·5	− 6·9	− 4·3	− 16·1	− 28·5
Under 5,000 ..	1	39·0	583	+ 21·0	− 14·7	− 13·3	− 3·7	− 2·8	− 16·3

CHAPTER III.

BIRTHPLACE.

Reference to statistics.

IMPERIAL Table VI gives particulars of the birthplace of the population. The one subsidiary table appended at the end of the chapter shows the persons born in Coorg and enumerated outside Coorg, in some of the Provinces and States.

Emigrations.

2. Emigration on an appreciable scale is not possible in Coorg as not only are the majority of the natural population agriculturists and as such closely attached to their cultivated lands but also they have no social or marital relationship with any class of people outside the Province. The bulk of the emigrants are found chiefly in Mysore and to a certain extent in the Presidency of Madras. They are all either prosecuting their studies or employees of Government or private persons. The statement at the end of this chapter is not complete and particularly the more important information about the number of such persons in Madras is not known, owing to retrenched sorting there. The number of emigrants according to this statement is 3,222 and presuming that the emigrants in the Madras Presidency are approximately 800 in number, the total will be close on 4,000. Persons born and enumerated in Coorg number 124,609. The natural population of Coorg will, therefore, be approximately 128,609 against 132,726 in 1921.

Immigrants.

3. Coming to immigrants, it is seen that they number 38,718 in 1931, compared to 33,937 in 1921. The decrease in the natural population is made up by the increase in the immigrant population. These conclusions are based on the assumption that a person's birthplace is ordinarily his normal residence with the notable exception of children born to some of the immigrant labourers, who, once they leave Coorg, do not ordinarily come back at all. Exceptions are not very common. The immigrants from Madras Presidency and Mysore have increased by roughly 3,000 and 2,000 respectively.

4. There has been a further decrease among persons born in Europe, the figure for 1931 being 72 against 83 in 1921, but the number of persons born in Asiatic provinces discloses a rise from 7 to 13 during the decade.

Emigrants from Coorg.

Persons born in Coorg and enumerated in			
Provinces, States and Agencies.	Persons.	M.	F.
1	2	3	4
Ajmer-Merwara ..	1	..	1
Andaman and Nicobar	7	7	..
Assam	1	..	1
Baluchistan	2	1	1
Bihar and Orissa ..	6	6	..
Bombay	144	120	24
Burma	2	..	2
Central India Agency..	1	..	1
Central Provinces and Berar	254	35	219
Cochin	2	1	1
Mysore	2,703	1,320	1,383
Rajputana	2	2	..
Travancore	8	4	4
United Provinces ..	89	85	4

CHAPTER IV.

AGE.

Reference to statistics. THIS chapter is devoted to the analysis of the age returns. The statistics regarding age distribution of the population are embodied in Imperial Table VII; the age-distribution of certain selected communities in Imperial Table VIII; and at the end of this chapter are appended subsidiary tables in which the figures are so re-arranged in proportional figures as to provide for comparative study of the salient features of the statistics.

Value of the statistics. 2. The instructions to the enumerators for filling in the age-column of the census schedule were to enter the nearest whole number of years on the 26th February 1931 and to record the age of infants less than six months as 0 and of those above six months and below one year as one year. The instructions were made sufficiently clear by holding classes, but, as usual, the results obtained do not appear to be quite satisfactory. It is ignorance rather than intentional mis-statement of age, which is the chief source of error in age-statistics. The bulk of the people having so little idea of their real age, give such ridiculous answers when questioned regarding it, that the enumerators have no other alternative than to record the age by sheer guess-work from the facial appearance and constitutional build of the person concerned. In Coorg, most of the enumerators being fairly well educated and being local people well acquainted with the people to be enumerated by them, it is presumed that their guesses about age, except in the cases of forest tribes, depressed classes and floating coolie population, might not have been wide of the mark. The common form of inaccuracy is, as usual, to give out ages in the multiples of 5 and 10 and the tendency to overstate or understate the age at certain periods of life is also not uncommon. Unmarried girls, who have attained the age of puberty, and bachelors and widowers intending to re-marry, who are approaching the meridian of life, often understate there age. Besides, old people and their young wives are prone to mis-state their age, perhaps to minimise the social disadvantages attendant on the disparity of their age. Excluding the large number of those, who have no real knowledge of their age, it may be said that intentional mis-statements are more common than unintentional ones. Another factor, which considerably affects the age-distribution is the inclusion in the return of approximately 38,000 immigrants, the majority of whom belong to the prime of life.

3. As it is not possible for a layman to eliminate the effects of these inaccuracies and as it will, as usual, be dealt with by the Government Actuary, the direct results deducible from the absolute figures of age-distribution of the population as obtained at the last census, are dealt with below. In Imperial Table VII, the figures of age-distribution of the population are given for each year of life up to 5, and then for quinquennial periods up to 70, with a single column for persons aged 70 and over. The total number for the 0–5 period is the largest of the total figures of all the other quinquennium periods. In the age-period 15–40, there are 45,087 males and 33,061 females, against 43,588 males and 32,495 females in 1921. Out of the floating coolie population of approximately 38,000, a substantial majority belong to the prime of life among both the sexes and this accounts for the unusual preponderance in Coorg of persons belonging to the age-period 15–40. According to the theory of the Swedish statistician Sundbärg, the number of persons aged 15–50, in all western countries, is uniformally about half the total population and it is said that this conclusion holds good in India, except for local variations. The fact that persons aged 15–40, represents 48 per cent and those aged 15–50, 57 per cent of the population in Coorg is attributed to the presence of a large number of immigrants in the prime of life. The number aged below fifteen comes to 57,092 or 35 per cent, and those aged over forty, 28,037 or 17 per cent of the population. Since the average age of a person in India is shorter than in other countries, the period 15–40, is taken into account instead of 15–50. The proportion of children indicates the progress of population, while that of old persons, affords some guide to longevity. As regards Coorg, it is not possible to take the percentage of 35

for children as a definite indication of any progress of population, as it is quite probable that the number of children below 15 might have risen owing to the inclusion of children belonging to immigrant labour classes. Even allowing a sufficient margin for this, it may not be incorrect to say that there may be an increase of population. Similarly it has to be admitted that the percentage of 17 for persons belonging to the age-period of 40 and over includes an appreciable number of immigrants and this coupled with the decrease of persons of the age of 50 and over is a disquieting feature, as it distinctly indicates a curtailment of the span of life. This feature becomes all the more vivid, if the number aged above 60 years is taken into consideration, inasmuch as there is no probability of any appreciable number of outsiders being included in this number. This figure comes to 4,921 against 6,138 in 1921 and 5,668 in 1911.

Age distribution.

4. According to Subsidiary Table *v*, the proportion of children under 10 to 100 persons aged 15–40 has fallen by 3·1 per cent during the decade but has increased by 3·5 per cent when compared with the figures for 1911. Similarly, the proportion of children under 10 per 100 married females aged 15–40 has gone down by 11·1 during the decade. In other words, for every 100 married females aged 15–40, there are 159·0 children under 10, against 171·1 in 1921 and this is partly due to the proportion of married females aged 15–40 to 100 females of all ages rising to 33·0 from 31·0 in 1921. While the married females of reproductive age have slightly increased, children per 100 females of that category have decreased. The explanation is that there has been a decrease in births and a high death-rate among children below 1 year. The following table shows the number of males and females from 1901 onwards in four different age-periods.

	0–5		10–15		20–25		30–35	
Year.	Males.	Females.	Males.	Females.	Males.	Females.	Males.	Females.
1931 ..	9,668	9,854	9,993	8,961	9,879	8,112	9,175	6,041
1921 ..	10,154	10,537	9,521	8,610	8,956	7,587	8,706	6,023
1911 ..	9,775	9,985	10,226	9,022	11,034	8,635	9,358	6,309
1901 ..	9,571	9,894	11,885	10,385	10,153	8,311	10,739	6,742

Persons, in the 0–5 group in 1921, when placed in group 10–15 in 1931, lost 161 males and 1,576 females. The loss of males can be traced to normal death-rate, but the abnormal decrease of females can be ascribed partly to increased death-rate but mostly to removal from the Province of children belonging to the immigrants. Again, persons in group 10–15 in 1921, when placed in group 20–25 in 1931, gained 358 males and lost 498 females. This is attributed mainly to influx of immigrants in the prime of life, who are mostly males, making allowance for the usual deaths. Lastly, those in the groups of 20–25 in 1921 when placed in group 30–35 gained 290 males and lost 1.546 females.

Births and deaths.

5. The birth and death-rates per mille during the decade are shown in Subsidiary Tables *vii* and *viii* and the death-rate per mille by sex and age in Subsidiary Table *ix*. The year 1921 records the highest birth-rate and the year 1924, the highest death-rate. On the other hand, the years 1928 and 1929 record the lowest birth and death-rates respectively. The preponderance of female death-rates over that of males during the reproductive age-period still continues.

Mean age.

6. The mean age refers to the average age of persons who were alive on the date of census, which works out to 24·97 for males and 23·16 for females against 25 and 24 respectively in 1921 according to Subsidiary Table *i*. But the mean age calculated according to the latest instructions from the Census Commissioner comes to 25·45 for males and 23·64 for females.

Age distribution by sex and religion.

7. The distribution of 10,000 of each sex and religion is detailed in Subsidiary Table *ii* for six censuses. The figures for Hindus cannot be compared with advantage since forest tribes considered as animists in 1921 have been considered as Hindus this time. Muhammadans under age group 0–5 have lost considerably among females but they have gained substantially in males in the age-period 20–40. Among Christians females under 0–5 group have decreased while there is an increase among both the sexes in the age-periods 15–20 and 20–40.

i.—*Age Distribution of* 10,000 *of each sex in the province.*

Age.	1931.		1921.		1911.		1901.		1891.		1881.	
	M.	F.	M.	F.	M.	F.	M.	F.	M.	F.	M.	F.
1	2	3	4	5	6	7	8	9	10	11	12	13
Total ..	*10,000*	*10,000*	*10,000*	*10,000*	*10,000*	*10,000*	*10,000*	*10,000*	*10,000*	*10,000*	*10,000*	*10,000*
0–1	235	300	222	287	216	268	275	351	221	286	205	280
0–2	241	302	128	167	141	186	81	104	151	197	130	173
2–3	211	278	261	329	220	292	205	259	251	330	136	187
3–4	190	244	265	336	218	276	182	250	263	354	182	249
4–5	190	231	258	298	210	263	212	267	228	288	186	237
0–5	1,067	1,355	1,134	1,417	1,005	1,285	955	1,231	1,114	1,455	839	1,126
5–10	1,052	1,249	1,039	1,276	977	1,225	1,121	1,393	1,146	1,388	1,113	1,421
10–15	1,103	1,232	1,064	1,158	1,051	1,161	1,185	1,293	941	988	1,133	1,166
15–20	1,008	1,032	931	884	1,041	1,052	972	964	988	1,031	1,152	1,101
20–25	1,091	1,115	1,001	1,021	1,134	1,111	1,013	1,034	1,093	1,121	1,144	1,177
25–30	1,075	980	1,117	1,055	1,203	1,031	1,218	1,084	1,277	1,104	1,310	1,184
30–35	1,013	830	973	810	962	812	1,071	839	1,032	818	1,078	855
35–40	791	587	848	601	809	567	787	543	767	540	781	546
40–45	619	469	595	486	646	531	643	527	605	529	575	480
45–50	416	345	439	348	408	331	347	285	364	269	311	256
50–55	307	277	340	356	329	362	316	350	314	327	275	291
55–60	181	196	181	169	156	152	130	130	131	115	96	99
60–65	134	156	180	211	150	199						
65–70	65	75	69	80	53	67	242	327	228	315	193	298
70 and over	78	102	89	128	76	114						
Mean age ..	24·97	23·16	25	24	25	24	25	23	24	23	24	23

ii.—*Age Distribution of* 10,000 *of each sex and religion in the province.*

Age.	1931.		1921.		1911.		1901.		1891.		1881.	
	M.	F.	M.	F.	M.	F.	M.	F.	M.	F.	M.	F.
1	2	3	4	5	6	7	8	9	10	11	12	13
HINDU ..	*10,000*	*10,000*	*10,000*	*10,000*	*10,000*	*10,000*	*10,000*	*10,000*	*10,000*	*10,000*	*10,000*	*10,000*
0–5	1,110	1,366	1,138	1,385	974	1,244	984	1,239	1,152	1,465	1,089	1,420
5–10	1,090	1,259	1,060	1,279	983	1,224	1,148	1,405	1,175	1,402	914	1,148
10–15	1,125	1,236	1,076	1,207	1,069	1,223	1,198	1,304	955	996	1,153	1,181
15–20	986	1,025	940	903	1,063	1,072	964	959	982	1,039	1,149	1,099
20–40	3,888	3,496	3,919	3,422	4,111	3,454	4,053	3,483	4,114	3,562	4,264	3,749
40–60	1,523	1,286	1,523	1,370	1,522	1,393	1,412	1,285	1,392	1,229	1,240	1,112
60 and over	278	332	344	434	278	390	241	325	230	307	191	291
MUSLIM ..	*10,000*	*10,000*	*10,000*	*10,000*	*10,000*	*10,000*	*10,000*	*10,000*	*10,000*	*10,000*	*10,000*	*10,000*
0–5	694	1,243	693	1,345	682	1,155	647	1,114	689	1,342	685	1,253
5–10	750	1,148	671	1,188	686	1,195	833	1,279	848	1,258	723	1,060
10–15	942	1,204	993	1,079	1,050	1,022	1,095	1,157	857	876	970	993
15–20	1,201	1,132	1,117	872	1,165	1,011	1,073	975	1,062	934	1,212	1,111
20–40	4,667	3,674	4,511	3,609	4,546	3,611	4,479	3,646	4,730	3,807	4,759	3,871
40–60	1,504	1,276	1,662	1,384	1,574	1,526	1,609	1,431	1,593	1,363	1,419	1,294
60 and over	242	323	353	523	297	480	264	398	221	420	232	418
CHRISTIAN ..	*10,000*	*10,000*	*10,000*	*10,000*	*10,000*	*10,000*	*10,000*	*10,000*	*10,000*	*10,000*	*10,000*	*10,000*
0–5	1,008	1,173	1,050	1,449	987	1,149	845	1,167	1,108	1,371	1,014	1,293
5–10	888	1,117	940	1,125	911	1,155	1,045	1,357	1,098	1,221	788	966
10–15	973	1,138	1,016	1,042	831	1,040	1,251	1,333	655	971	868	995
15–20	1,017	1,032	779	794	982	1,136	943	935	937	984	1,065	1,191
20–40	4,139	3,738	3,872	3,478	4,023	3,644	3,977	3,509	4,386	3,858	4,766	4,016
40–60	1,613	1,435	1,939	1,608	1,853	1,455	1,695	1,363	1,623	1,280	1,341	1,285
60 and over	362	367	404	504	413	421	244	336	193	315	158	254

iii.—*Age Distribution of* 1,000 *of each sex in certain castes.*

Castes.	Males—Number per mille aged.						Females—Number per mille aged.					
	0–6.	7–13.	14–16.	17–23.	24–43.	44 and over.	0–6.	7–13.	14–16	17–23.	24–43.	44 and over.
1	2	3	4	5	6	7	8	9	10	11	12	13
Amma Kodaga	164	155	89	137	300	155	194	185	48	158	270	145
Arya Vaisya	150	180	60	140	340	130	235	180	90	180	189	126
Bant	79	108	61	144	483	125	183	159	56	143	336	123
Boya	133	142	66	137	438	84	175	124	46	180	360	115
Brahman (Kanarese) ..	121	165	70	158	330	156	157	192	70	133	277	171
Gauda	159	167	62	131	335	146	190	184	69	138	291	128
Golla	152	166	59	118	353	152	169	199	52	117	294	169
Holeya	130	141	54	146	416	113	163	193	22	222	296	104
Kodaga	178	199	70	125	281	147	177	199	72	137	270	145
Kudiya	193	181	63	122	311	130	219	161	32	133	305	150
Kuruba	172	143	54	103	368	160	188	157	54	141	359	101
Labbai	119	103	71	119	445	143	152	152	65	174	315	142
Lingayat	125	189	77	119	349	141	137	202	75	133	303	150
Madiga	205	131	82	82	402	98	137	274	42	147	305	95
Mapilla	77	106	79	178	455	105	158	177	70	165	325	105
Moratha	22	69	69	167	542	131	67	122	67	167	405	172
Nayar	22	36	33	188	584	137	180	157	84	135	348	96
Pale	63	107	65	161	509	95	148	157	57	182	378	78
Paraiyan	120	130	54	152	462	82	180	128	38	135	455	64
Panchama	113	148	72	125	430	112	153	180	61	151	358	97
Telaga	141	211	56	141	282	169	188	131	58	116	348	159
Vakkaliya	123	158	83	144	371	121	148	185	73	137	317	140
Yerava	181	138	52	91	378	160	202	142	48	134	362	112

iv.—Proportion of Children under 14 *and of persons over* 43 *to those aged* 14–43 *in certain castes ; also of married females aged* 14–43 *per* 100 *females.*

Caste.	Proportion of children of both sexes per 100 — Persons aged 14–43.	Proportion of children of both sexes per 100 — Married females aged 14–43.	Proportion of persons over 43 per 100 aged 14–43. — Males.	Proportion of persons over 43 per 100 aged 14–43. — Females.	Number of married females aged 14–43. — Per 100 females of all ages.
1	2	3	4	5	6
Amma Kodaga	69	225	29	31	31
Arya Vaisya	75	176	24	27	41
Bant	38	181	18	23	37
Boya	47	165	13	20	35
Brahman (Kanarese)	60	207	28	36	33
Gauda	68	214	28	26	34
Golla	68	219	29	36	35
Holeya	52	196	18	19	37
Kodaga	79	265	31	30	29
Kudiya	78	223	26	32	33
Kuruba	61	164	30	18	44
Labbai	43	160	23	25	38
Lingayat	62	194	26	29	30
Madiga	69	242	17	19	35
Mappilla	35	169	15	19	44
Maratha	17	78	17	27	48
Nayar	13	163	17	17	43
Pale	31	135	13	13	48
Paraiyan	43	118	12	10	51
Panchama	49	166	18	17	40
Telaga	67	209	35	31	33
Vakkaliya	54	204	20	27	32
Yerava	62	158	31	21	44

v.—Proportion of Children under 10 *and of persons over* 60 *to those aged* 15–40 *; also of married females aged* 15–40 *per* 100 *females.*

Province.	Proportion of children of both sexes per 100 — Persons aged 15–40.					Married females aged 15–40.					Proportion of persons over 60 per 100 persons aged 15–40. — 1931.		1921.	
	1931.	1921.	1911.	1901.	1891.	1931.	1921.	1911.	1901.	1891.	M.	F.	M.	F.
1	2	3	4	5	6	7	8	9	10	11	12	13	14	15
Coorg	48·8	51·9	45·3	48·4	51·2	159·0	171·1	155·7	164·4	162·6	5·6	7·3	6·9	9·6

Province.	Proportion of persons over 60 per 100 persons aged 15–40—*cont.* — 1911.		1901.		1891.		Number of married females aged 15–40 per 100 females of all ages.				
	M.	F.	M.	F.	M.	F.	1931.	1921.	1911.	1901.	1891.
	16	17	18	19	20	21	22	23	24	25	26
Coorg	5·4	8·3	4·8	7·3	4·4	6·8	33·0	31·0	32·1	31·7	34·7

v-a.—Proportion of Children under 10 *and of persons over* 60 *to those aged* 15–40 *in certain religions ; also of married females aged* 15–40 *per* 100 *females.*

Religion.	Proportion of children of both sexes per 100 — Persons aged 15–40.	Married females aged 15–40.	Proportion of persons over 60 per 100 persons aged 15–40. — Males.	Females	Number of married females aged 15–40, per 100 females of all ages.
1	2	3	4	5	6
Hindu	50·8	161·5	5·7	7·3	32·6
Muslim	32·3	132·8	4·1	6·7	38·1
Christian	41·2	146·5	7·0	7·7	34·1

vi.—Variation in population at certain age-periods.

Province.	Period.	Variation per cent in population (Increase +, Decrease —) — All ages.	0–10.	10–15.	15–40.	40–60.	60 and over.
1	2	3	4	5	6	7	8
Coorg	1921–1931 ..	— 0·3	— 3·4	+ 4·5	+ 2·7	— 3·5	—19·8
	1911–1921 ..	— 6·4	+ 1·8	— 5·8	—11·1	— 6·4	+ 8·3
	1901–1911 ..	— 3·1	— 7·4	—13·6	— 1·1	+ 3·6	+12·1
	1891–1901 ..	+ 4·4	— 3·9	+33·8	+ 1·8	+ 7·2	+ 8·4
	1881–1891 ..	— 2·9	+10·6	— 8·7	— 8·3	+ 8·1	+ 9·4

vii.—Reported Birthrate per mille during the decade 1921–30.

Number of births per mille of total population in

Province.	1921. M.	1921. F.	1922. M.	1922. F.	1923. M.	1923. F.	1924. M.	1924. F.	1925. M.	1925. F.	1926. M.	1926. F.	1927. M.	1927. F.	1928. M.	1928. F.	1929. M.	1929. F.	1930. M.	1930. F.	Average birth-rate per mille of total population during the decade. P.	M.	F.
1	2	3	4	5	6	7	8	9	10	11	12	13	14	15	16	17	18	19	20	21	22	23	24
Coorg	14·0	13·4	13·8	12·3	13·3	12·3	10·9	10·3	9·7	9·2	11·8	11·0	10·1	9·1	9·2	8·8	11·5	10·7	12·3	11·3	22·5	11·7	10·8

viii.—Reported Deathrate per mille during the decade 1921–30.

Number of deaths per mille of population of each sex in

Province.	1921. M.	1921. F.	1922. M.	1922. F.	1923. M.	1923. F.	1924. M.	1924. F.	1925. M.	1925. F.	1926. M.	1926. F.	1927. M.	1927. F.	1928. M.	1928. F.	1929. M.	1929. F.	1930. M.	1930. F.	Average deathrate per mille of population of each sex during the decade. P.	M.	F.
1	2	3	4	5	6	7	8	9	10	11	12	13	14	15	16	17	18	19	20	21	22	23	24
Coorg	28·0	29·3	32·9	36·6	27·7	30·9	39·0	43·5	30·9	30·7	34·2	34·1	30·9	31·9	30·5	32·1	22·6	25·1	24·2	26·5	31·0	30·1	32·1

ix.—Reported Deathrate per mille in Coorg by sex and age.

Age.	Average of decade 1921–30. M.	F.	1923. M.	F.	1925. M.	F.	1927. M.	F.	1929. M.	F.
1	2	3	4	5	6	7	8	9	10	11
All ages ..	*30*	*32*	*28*	*31*	*31*	*31*	*31*	*32*	*23*	*25*
Under 1 year ..	250	220	237	206	232	209	222	176	219	180
1– 5	35	33	32	32	38	35	26	24	21	19
5–10	14	14	13	12	13	12	19	16	11	11
10–15	10	10	9	11	10	7	11	10	8	10
15–20	17	21	17	21	15	16	15	18	13	22
20–30	21	25	19	23	24	25	21	24	16	22
30–40	26	30	22	31	27	28	29	34	19	23
40–50	33	34	33	34	35	31	35	42	25	27
50–60	47	44	41	45	49	46	58	54	35	28
60 and over ..	66	60	61	55	69	67	74	76	43	37

x.—Reported deaths from certain diseases per mille of each sex.

Actual number of deaths from

Year.	Fever. Males.	Fever. Females.	Cholera. Males.	Cholera. Females.	Smallpox. Males.	Smallpox. Females.	Plague. Males.	Plague. Females.
1	2	3	4	5	6	7	8	9
Total ..	*21,110*	*19,755*	*19*	*16*	*106*	*118*	*20*	*14*
1921	1,873	1,742	..	..	3	3	1	..
1922	2,333	2,271	2	2	1	..	6	2
1923	1,974	1,908	..	..	6	12	..	..
1924	2,845	2,758	11	13	39	30	2	1
1925	2,208	1,908	3	1	8	18	..	..
1926	2,359	2,082	2	..	..	1	4	7
1927	2,129	1,963	..	..	3	3	5	2
1928	2,168	1,989	..	..	32	40	..	..
1929	1,563	1,548	1	..	12	11	..	1
1930	1,658	1,586	..	..	2	..	2	1
Average annual rate per mille of population of each sex ..	*23·6*	*26·6*	*0·02*	*0·02*	*0·1*	*0·02*	*0·02*	*0·02*

CHAPTER V.

SEX.

Reference to statistics. The distribution of population by sex is maintained in all the Census Tables and the statistics discussed in this chapter are contained chiefly in Imperial Table VII, in which the figures of sex at different age periods by religion and civil condition are given and in Imperial Table VIII, which exhibits figures of civil condition by age for selected communities. The proportion of females per 1,000 males at different age periods by religion at each of the last four censuses is illustrated in Subsidiary Table *i*. The number of births and deaths since 1921 among both the sexes is dealt with in Subsidiary Table *iii* and deaths of each sex at different ages in Subsidiary Table *iv*. Lastly, the proportion of females at different age periods in certain selected castes and tribes are shown in Subsidiary Table *ii*.

Sex population. 2. The preponderance of males over females in India, unlike western countries, is generally attributed to imperfection of enumeration but that this inference is fallacious has been sufficiently explained in the All-India Census report for 1911. In Coorg, as in India in general, there is an excess of males over females. The possibility of omission of certain females in the census schedule is extremely remote and there can be little doubt that sex figures are accurate.

Summary of statistics. 3. The population of the province consists of 90,575 males and 72,752 females, which means that there are 803 females to every 1,000 males, as against 831 in 1921.

Sex proportion. 4. The proportion of females in this province is lower than in the provinces and States shown below :—

Provinces and States.	Females for 1,000 males.	Provinces and States.	Females for 1,000 males.
India	940	Baroda State	942
Madras	1,025	Bengal	924
Hyderabad	961	Bombay	908
Mysore	955	Coorg	803

Among the three principal religions, the proportion varies widely, as seen from the figures tabulated below :—

Religions.	Females for 1,000 males.	Religions.	Females for 1,000 males.
All Religions	803	Muslims	542
Hindus	835	Christians	702

Taking into account only persons born and enumerated in Coorg the ratio is 919 females to 1,000 males. The lower proportion of females is attributable to the immigrant labourers and traders numbering roughly 38,000, among whom males represent almost double the number of females. The names of a few immigrant classes, with the sex proportions among them, are given below to substantiate the above conclusion ;—

Immigrant classes.	Males.	Females.	Proportion of females per 1,000 males.	Immigrant classes.	Males.	Females.	Proportion of females per 1,000 males.
Nayar	1,100	178	162	Pale	2,128	1,064	500
Bant	872	497	570	Vokkaliga ..	4,233	3,715	878
Mappilla ..	6,051	2,753	455	Christians ..	2,015	1,415	707

The very low proportion among Muslims is evidently due to the large number of male immigrants among them, Mappillas alone showing an excess of 3,298 males over females, for a total population of 8,804. Among Hindus, there are 1,028 females for every 1,000 males for the age-period 0–5. The sex proportions of some of the important indigenous communities are noted below in the order of their importance :—

Communities.	Males.	Females.	Communities.	Males.	Females.
Kodava	20,752	20,274	Yerava	6,763	6,047
Gauda	7,388	6,628	Kuruba	3,710	3,157
Panchama ..	10,971	8,600			

5. The sex proportion in Mercara works out to 749 and in Virajpet 583 for every 1,000 males. The low sex ratio is due to most of the trading classes, conducting business in these towns, leaving their womenfolk in their native homes. Virajpet being a moie busy trading centre than Mercara, the number of such businessmen preponderate there and this accounts for a lower female sex ratio than in Mercara. Taking the talukwar sex-ratios into consideration, there are 811 and 796 females for every 1,000 males in North Coorg and South Coorg taluks respectively.

Comparison with vital statistics.

6. It is seen from Subsidiary Table *v* that during the last decade, the number of female births and deaths per 1,000 male births and deaths was 928 and 884 respectively against 951 and 867 for the decade 1911–20. While the female births have diminished by 23 per mille, the deaths of males have risen by 17 per mille. This explains the decrease of the female ratio per 1,000 males, from 831 in 1921 to 803 in 1931. Subsidiary Table *vi*, shows that during the past decade the number of deaths below 1 year was excessive as usual, deaths among males exceeding those of females.

i.—Number of Females per 1,000 males at different age-periods by religions at each of the last four censuses.

Age.	All religions.				Hindu.				Muslim.				Christian.			
	1931.	1921.	1911.	1901.	1931.	1921.	1911.	1901.	1931.	1921.	1911.	1901.	1931.	1921.	1911.	1901.
1	2	3	4	5	6	7	8	9	10	11	12	13	14	15	16	17
Total of all ages (actual population)	*803*	*831*	*799*	*801*	*835*	*859*	*808*	*818*	*541*	*559*	*565*	*609*	*702*	*836*	*789*	*799*
0–1	1,028	1,071	990	1,020	1,034	1,089	994	1,019	1,000	1,314	978	1,072	800	1,158	1,114	1,152
1–2	1,005	1,083	1,056	1,035	1,012	1,101	1,061	1,026	1,000	889	902	1,096	750	1,500	786	958
2–3	1,057	1,049	1,060	1,017	1,067	1,067	1,074	1,014	1,016	1,103	1,083	975	814	892	875	1,231
3–4	1,033	1,054	1,009	1,100	1,045	1,058	1,039	1,100	921	1,154	908	1,000	886	1,372	889	1,071
4–5	972	958	1,002	1,011	979	948	1,001	1,003	877	979	889	1,121	875	1,042	872	1,028
Total 0–5	*1,019*	*1,038*	*1,021*	*1,034*	*1,028*	*1,046*	*1,032*	*1,030*	*968*	*1,085*	*956*	*1,049*	*818*	*1,154*	*918*	*1,104*
5–10	954	1,020	1,002	996	965	1,037	1,006	1,001	827	991	984	935	883	1,000	1,000	1,037
10–15	897	904	882	874	917	964	925	890	691	608	550	644	821	858	988	852
15–20	823	789	807	795	868	825	815	814	509	436	491	554	712	852	913	793
20–25	821	847	783	819	874	854	777	839	485	434	452	586	672	933	796	858
25–30	732	785	684	714	776	794	662	741	421	471	507	448	664	839	662	689
Total 0–30 ..	*874*	*900*	*855*	*868*	*907*	*923*	*859*	*884*	*602*	*608*	*602*	*656*	*755*	*942*	*866*	*881*
30–40	631	644	622	596	663	665	627	604	388	439	411	476	598	609	696	638
40–50	632	670	653	657	655	703	673	675	423	456	513	521	625	699	561	588
50–60	780	837	846	860	812	915	886	899	535	482	619	587	624	684	732	754
60 and over	965	1,028	1,089	1,084	997	1,084	1,136	1,103	722	827	916	920	712	1,043	805	1,100
Total 30 and over ..	*677*	*713*	*698*	*680*	*707*	*749*	*715*	*695*	*438*	*485*	*506*	*534*	*618*	*690*	*671*	*669*

ii.—Number of Females per 1,000 males for certain selected castes and tribes.

Castes.	All ages.	0–6.	7–13.	14–16.	17–23.	24–43.	44 and over.
1	2	3	4	5	6	7	8
Amma Kodaga	982	1,164	1,173	533	1,130	881	923
Arya Vaisya	1,110	1,733	1,111	1,667	1,429	618	1,077
Bant	570	1,319	840	528	563	396	560
Boya	960	1,267	844	667	1,258	788	1,316
Brahman (Kanarese) ..	836	1,084	973	833	704	704	916
Gauda	897	1,074	989	996	941	780	787
Golla	799	886	958	706	794	667	886
Holeya	730	917	1,000	300	1,111	519	667
Kodaga	977	976	978	994	1,070	939	962
Kudiya	1,033	1,173	918	529	1,121	1,012	1,200
Kuruba	851	931	934	847	1,164	831	536
Labbai	730	933	1,077	667	1,067	518	722
Lingayat	1,252	1,369	1,333	1,220	1,408	1,091	1,327
Madiga	779	520	1,625	400	1,400	592	750
Mappilla	455	935	760	404	421	325	457
Maratha	500	1,500	880	480	500	374	660
Nayar	162	1,333	700	417	116	97	113
Pale	500	1,180	736	442	567	371	409
Paraiyan	848	1,273	833	600	750	835	667
Panchama	784	1,056	957	666	947	652	680
Telega	972	1,300	600	1,000	800	1,200	917
Vokkaliga	878	1,056	1,030	767	831	751	1,018
Yerava	894	998	917	834	1,317	855	528

iii.—Actual Number of Births and Deaths reported since 1921 in Coorg.

Year.	Number of births.			Number of deaths.			Difference between columns 3 and 4—excess of latter over former (+) defect (—).	Difference between columns 6 and 7—excess of latter over former (+) defect (—).	Difference between columns 2 and 5—excess of former over latter (+) defect (—).	Number of female births per 1,000 of male births.	Number of female deaths per 1,000 of male deaths.
	P.	M.	F.	P.	M.	F.					
1	2	3	4	5	6	7	8	9	10	11	12
Total 1921–1930 ..	*36,818*	*19,094*	*17,724*	*50,774*	*26,943*	*23,831*	— *1,370*	— *3,112*	—*13,956*	*928*	*884*
1921	4,494	2,300	2,194	4,679	2,503	2,176	— 106	— 327	— 185	954	869
1922	4,272	2,262	2,010	5,668	2,944	2,724	— 252	— 220	— 1,396	889	925
1923	4,197	2,184	2,013	4,775	2,477	2,298	— 171	— 179	— 578	922	928
1924	3,474	1,792	1,682	6,726	3,500	3,226	— 110	— 274	— 3,252	939	922
1925	3,093	1,587	1,506	5,049	2,765	2,284	+ 81	— 481	— 1,956	949	826
1926	3,728	1,927	1,801	5,599	3,062	2,537	— 126	— 525	— 1,871	935	829
1927	3,141	1,652	1,489	5,138	2,769	2,369	— 163	— 400	— 1,997	901	856
1928	2,940	1,501	1,439	5,110	2,727	2,383	— 62	— 344	— 2,170	959	874
1929	3,623	1,877	1,746	3,889	2,026	1,863	— 131	— 163	— 266	930	920
1930	3,856	2,012	1,844	4,141	2,170	1,971	— 168	— 199	— 285	917	908

iv.—Number of Deaths of each sex at different ages.

Age.	1921.		1922.		1923.		1924.		1925.		1926.		1927.		1928.		1929.		1930.		Total.		Average number of female deaths per 1,000 male deaths.
	M.	F.	M.	F.	M.	F.	M.	F.	M.	F.	M.	F.	M.	F.	M.	F.	M.	F.	M.	F.	M.	F.	
1	2	3	4	5	6	7	8	9	10	11	12	13	14	15	16	17	18	19	20	21	22	23	24
Total ..	*2,503*	*2,176*	*2,944*	*2,724*	*2,477*	*2,298*	*3,500*	*3,226*	*2,765*	*2,284*	*3,062*	*2,537*	*2,769*	*2,369*	*2,727*	*2,383*	*2,026*	*1,863*	*2,170*	*1,971*	*26,943*	*23,831*	*884*
0–1	512	499	602	562	472	440	562	588	462	446	557	499	442	375	419	425	485	384	511	472	4,974	4,690	943
1–5	290	304	430	454	264	267	465	465	308	297	308	268	213	200	199	191	169	162	192	183	2,838	2,791	983
5–10	109	128	129	150	117	118	162	166	121	115	148	159	181	152	151	119	100	101	110	90	1,328	1,293	974
10–15	86	55	92	91	87	91	109	89	99	58	85	72	108	83	135	105	72	89	80	91	953	824	865
15–20	135	117	141	143	139	135	197	186	125	103	184	150	126	120	152	180	107	142	109	136	1,415	1,412	998
20–30	347	352	419	414	365	359	480	504	447	390	492	431	399	370	376	425	306	346	307	342	3,938	3,933	999
30–40	399	252	436	324	357	329	545	404	441	293	495	342	477	361	486	351	311	245	323	243	4,270	3,144	736
40–50	243	179	271	206	308	212	407	269	325	193	332	231	327	263	359	251	231	108	233	164	3,031	2,136	705
50–60	206	153	227	202	189	175	295	262	229	180	246	176	271	210	222	161	165	110	142	101	2,192	1,730	789
60 and over ..	176	142	197	178	184	172	278	298	208	209	215	209	225	235	228	175	130	116	163	149	2,004	1,878	937

CHAPTER VI.

CIVIL CONDITION.

Reference to statistics. THE number of married, unmarried and widowed persons of each sex for the Province by age and by religion is given in Imperial Tables VII and VIII. The four subsidiary tables appended at the end of this chapter show the following important features of the statistics :—

(i) the distribution by civil condition of 1,000 of each sex, religion and main age period at each of the last five censuses,

(ii) the distribution by main age periods and civil condition of 1,000 of each sex and religion,

(iii) the proportion of sexes by civil condition at certain ages by religions,

(iv) the distribution by civil condition of 1,000 of each sex at certain ages for selected castes.

Definition of 'married.' 2. The instructions to enumerators were to record each person, whether infant, child or grown up, as married, unmarried or widowed exactly as the person described himself or herself to be. Divorced persons were treated as widowed. The performance of the full formal ceremony of marriage according to the recognized social customs obtaining in each community was considered to be the test of marriage. During the decade the marriage customs did not undergo any important change in any community. In Coorg, post-puberty marriages immediately followed by cohabitation are prevalent among the dominent communities and child marriages which are nothing more than 'inviolable betrothals' and in which some time elapses before the consummation takes place, are in vogue among Brahmans, a section of Muhammadans and a few other minor communities. The social interest requires the figures relating only to consummated marriages, but no attempts at obtaining these figures are made since at best they will be of doubtful value owing to the considerable difficulties in obtaining the information.

Variations 1891-1931. 3. Of the total population of 163,327 enumerated in the Province, 82,535 were returned as unmarried, 64,417 as married and 16,375 as widowed against 83,944, 62,739 and 17,155, respectively, in 1921. The table below indicates the variations among the three forms of civil condition during the past five censuses as distributed per mille of males and females of all ages and religions :—

Year.			Per 1,000 males.			Per 1,000 females.		
			Unmarried.	Married.	Widowed.	Unmarried.	Married.	Widowed.
1931	..	..	554	393	53	444	396	160
1921	..	..	562	386	52	453	379	168
1911	..	..	554	400	46	440	387	173
1901	..	..	555	396	49	446	378	176
1891	..	..	531	430	39	423	410	167

Civil condition by age periods. 4. The figures summarised from Imperial Table VII and tabulated in next page show the figures of civil condition for each sex in the main age groups. Considerably more than half the males (554 : 1,000) are unmarried, slightly less than one-nineteenth (53 : 1,000) are widowers, while 393 males to every 1,000 or a little less than two-fifths are married. Turning to females, nearly 40 out of every 100 are married, slightly less than one-sixth are widowed and the rest are unmarried. At the age period 20–40, there are 12,364 unmarried males while at the period 15–40 there are only 4,944 unmarried females. This great disparity which is not perceptible below the age of 15 is due to the inclusion of many immigrant males in the prime of life who are not accompanied by their wives. The civil condition at the age periods 15–20 and 20–40 is shown in the margin with similar figures for 1921.

Age.	1931 Males.			1931 Females.		
	M.	U.	W.	M.	U.	W.
15–20	859	8,232	38	4,064	3,241	205
20–40	21,715	12,364	1,879	19,920	1,703	3,928

Age.	1921. Males.			1921. Females.		
	M.	U.	W.	M.	U.	W.
15–20	345	7,972	13	2,541	3,877	158
20–40	20,649	12,920	1,689	20,529	1,524	3,871

M. = Married. U. = Unmarried. W. = Widowed.

Age.		Males.			Females.	
	Married.	Unmarried.	Widowed.	Married.	Unmarried.	Widowed.
0– 5 ..	11	9,657	..	21	9,831	2
5–10 ..	36	9,491	..	86	8,995	8
10–15 ..	66	9,925	2	493	8,442	26
15–20 ..	859	8,232	38	4,064	3,241	205
20–40 ..	21,715	12,364	1,879	19,920	1,703	3,928
40–60 ..	11,306	489	2,001	3,942	94	5,334
60 and over	1,589	54	861	309	17	2,091

Civil condition for selected communities.

5. In all three dominant religions of Hindu, Muslim and Christian, unmarried and married males are much in excess of the number of unmarried and married females, particularly in the age-period 20–40, and widows are over three times the number of widowers. Imperial Table VIII is new and shows civil condition for selected communities. The dominant community in Coorg is the Coorg or 'Kodaga'. Among them unmarried males exceed the number of unmarried females by 2,573 while the number of married males and females is almost equal (6,708 males and 6,888 females) and the number of widows is nearly three times the number of widowers. The next community in the order of importance, is the 'Gauda' and they also bear the same proportions as Coorg. A typical community consisting mostly of immigrants is the 'Mopla' among whom the number of unmarried males is almost thrice the number of unmarried females and the number of married males is double the number of married females. This vast difference is due to the fact that most of the males come to Coorg as immigrants either for trade or for work in the plantations or on roads, unaccompanied by their families.

Universality of marriage.

6. Marriage is recognized generally as a religious obligation and consequently the married state is the rule throughout Coorg as elsewhere in India. Among Hindus, who form 90 per cent of the population, every man is required to marry as a necessity enjoined by religion to beget a son to perform his funeral rites. Among Mussalmans also marriage is considered obligatory, though not for the same reasons as Hindus. Christians being hardly 2 per cent of the population their inclusion does not materially alter the position. The result is that at the age of 40 and over only 15 females and 60 males out of every 10,000 of that sex remain unmarried. (See Subsidiary Table *iii.*) The universality of marriage is clearly illustrated in the marginal diagram. The figures tabulated below give similar figures for the three main religions separately :—

Diagram showing the population per mille who are married at each age-period.

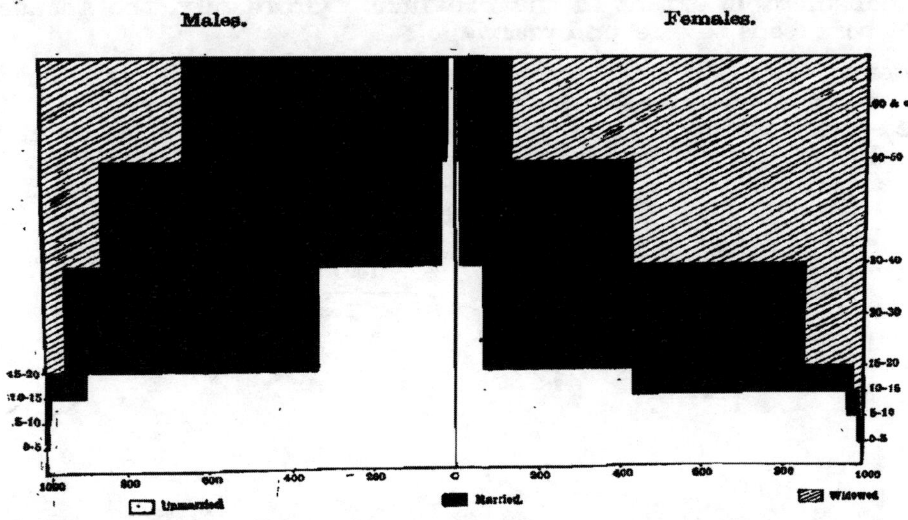

Religion.	Unmarried at 40 and over per 10,000 of population.		Religion.	Unmarried at 40 and over per 10,000 of population.	
	Males.	Females.		Males.	Females.
All Religions ..	60	15	Muslims	46	6
Hindus	60	14	Christians	124	85

The unmarried persons in all these cases are mostly those suffering from constitutional defects such as, infirmity and deformity; beggars, prostitutes, mendicants, etc. The unusually large percentage of unmarried persons among Christians is due among other causes to a large number of Europeans and also Indian Christians who have entered religious celibate orders being employed in Christian institutions in the Province.

Child Marriage.

7. The early age at which children in India are married is another striking feature of Indian statistics. This is undoubtedly a social evil and Coorg fortunately stands on a higher level than most of the Provinces in this respect inasmuch as early marriages, though not entirely unknown, are almost negligible in number. From time immemorial the main communities have been practising post-puberty marriages and in recent years there has been a growing tendency actuated by prudential considerations among all the communities to postpone the age of marriage still further. The operation of the Sarda Act had therefore no special effect in Coorg.

Civil condition by religion.

8. The proportion of married males and females in each religion in the first four quinquennial age-periods of life per mille of population is seen from the figures tabulated below :—

Age-period.	Males.			Females.		
	Hindus.	Muslims.	Christians.	Hindus.	Muslims.	Christians.
0– 5	1	..	..	2	3	..
5–10	4	3	..	9	23	..
10–15	7	5	5	50	129	39
15–20	96	87	68	526	720	541

No one below 10 years is married among Christians. There are a few cases among Muslims and Hindus but this number is negligible. The number of married persons below five years is 11 males and 21 females in 1931 against 34 males and 44 females in 1921. This indicates that the evil of early marriage is diminishing. It is indeed doubtful whether there were really 7 marriages among Coorgs and 2 among Gaudas, all below 6 years of age, as such occurrences are practically unknown among them. Polygamy, though permitted, is not practised to any considerable extent in the Province. Ordinarily, the absence of a child to a first wife leads to a second marriage.

Child widows.

9. The number of widows in any country depends largely on the number of child marriages performed, the great disparity of age between husband and wife and the prejudice against widow marriage. Since all these are very uncommon in Coorg, the number of widows in general and child widows in particular is insignificant. The figures tabulated below show the number of persons widowed in 1921 and 1931 below 15 years of age. There is a marked improvement for 1931.

Age-period.	1931.		1921.	
	Males.	Females.	Males.	Females.
0– 5	..	2	4	9
5–10	..	8	1	15
10–15	2	26	6	33

i.—Distribution by Civil Condition of 1,000 of each sex, religion and main age-period at each of the last five censuses.

Religion.	Sex and age.	Unmarried. 1931.	Unmarried. 1921.	Unmarried. 1911.	Unmarried. 1901.	Unmarried. 1801.	Married. 1931.	Married. 1921.	Married. 1911.	Married. 1901.	Married. 1891.	Widowed. 1931.	Widowed. 1921.	Widowed. 1911.	Widowed. 1901.	Widowed. 1891
	1	2	3	4	5	6	7	8	9	10	11	12	13	14	15	16
ALL RELIGIONS.	**Males**	**528**	**545**	**547**	**526**	**499**	**442**	**426**	**421**	**442**	**479**	**30**	**29**	**32**	**32**	**22**
	0–5	1,000	1,000	996	989	993	..	..	..	9	7	..	..	4	2	..
	5–10	997	1,000	996	997	999	3	..	4	3	1	..	..	..	..	..
	10–15	995	989	987	985	988	5	11	13	15	12	..	..	..	..	..
	15–20	909	960	960	940	027	87	40	40	57	72	4	..	..	3	1
	20–40	379	435	416	367	331	591	539	556	607	651	30	26	28	26	18
	40–60	25	38	36	32	35	904	896	868	876	901	71	66	96	92	64
	60 and over	37	27	20	27	56	782	797	776	785	799	181	176	204	188	145
	Females	**379**	**384**	**357**	**373**	**361**	**435**	**426**	**439**	**430**	**451**	**166**	**190**	**204**	**197**	**188**
	0–5	997	1,000	1,000	997	998	3	..	..	3	2	..	..	..	..	..
	5–10	977	1,000	999	997	992	23	..	11	3	8	..	..	..	..	..
	10–15	861	885	854	863	830	129	103	144	130	163	10	12	2	7	7
	15–20	234	317	265	268	209	720	644	693	692	764	46	39	42	40	27
	20–40	31	24	23	23	33	816	811	809	794	825	153	165	168	183	142
	40–60	3	6	7	4	9	410	421	431	374	331	587	573	562	622	660
	60 and over	6	8	4	..	..	96	123	72	87	35	898	869	924	913	965
HINDU.	**Males**	**567**	**549**	**545**	**575**	**542**	**387**	**393**	**411**	**385**	**417**	**46**	**58**	**44**	**40**	**41**
	0–5	1,000	1,000	1,000	1,000	990	..	..	..	..	10	..	..	..	..	..
	5–10	1,000	988	994	1,000	995	..	12	6	..	5	..	..	..	..	..
	10–15	995	994	982	992	1,000	5	6	18	8	..	..	..	..	..	..
	15–20	927	985	959	979	920	68	15	41	21	80	5	..	..	..	..
	20–40	420	414	395	390	360	542	537	572	572	606	38	49	33	38	34
	40–60	74	54	98	72	89	800	830	796	833	802	126	116	106	95	109
	60 and over	14	57	61	120	27	726	672	671	540	541	260	271	268	340	432
	Females	**423**	**462**	**442**	**466**	**420**	**422**	**391**	**389**	**369**	**393**	**155**	**147**	**169**	**165**	**187**
	0–5	1,000	1,000	1,000	995	995	..	..	..	5	5	..	..	..	..	..
	5–10	1,000	994	1,000	1,000	995	..	6	..	..	5	..	..	..	..	..
	10–15	963	1,000	982	992	1,000	37	..	18	8	..	..	..	..	..	..
	15–20	438	591	522	562	380	541	400	472	412	593	21	9	6	26	27
	20–40	83	119	130	85	80	762	782	737	758	745	155	99	133	157	175
	40–60	54	82	26	22	26	483	437	425	404	303	463	481	549	574	671
	60 and over	19	14	30	..	21	212	301	61	127	21	769	685	909	873	958
MUSLIM.	**Males**	**554**	**562**	**554**	**555**	**531**	**393**	**386**	**400**	**396**	**430**	**53**	**52**	**46**	**49**	**39**
	0–5	909	996	999	097	996	1	4	1	3	4	..	..	..	..	..
	5–10	996	996	998	996	995	4	4	2	4	5	..	..	..	..	..
	10–15	993	991	990	988	982	7	8	10	12	18	..	1	..	..	..
	15–20	902	957	946	939	890	94	41	53	59	106	4	2	1	2	4
	20–40	344	366	362	327	291	604	586	625	620	672	52	48	13	53	37
	40–60	35	34	36	36	33	820	822	829	823	846	145	144	135	141	121
	60 and over	21	25	22	18	20	635	655	676	684	715	344	320	302	298	265
	Females	**444**	**453**	**440**	**446**	**423**	**396**	**379**	**387**	**378**	**410**	**160**	**168**	**173**	**176**	**167**
	0–5	998	995	999	998	994	2	4	1	2	5	..	1	..	..	1
	5–10	990	992	997	096	990	9	7	3	4	9	1	1	..	..	1
	10–15	942	955	937	928	884	55	41	61	69	112	3	4	2	3	4
	15–20	432	590	568	504	368	541	389	411	465	607	27	23	21	31	25
	20–40	67	60	57	43	41	779	792	787	778	794	154	156	156	179	165
	40–60	10	12	6	9	12	421	421	401	544	375	569	567	593	447	613
	60 and over	7	13	9	7	7	128	128	92	95	98	865	850	899	898	895
CHRISTIAN.	**Males**	**557**	**570**	**560**	**557**	**534**	**387**	**377**	**393**	**392**	**426**	**56**	**53**	**47**	**51**	**40**
	0–5	999	997	1,000	998	996	1	3	..	2	4	..	..	..	..	..
	5–10	996	996	998	995	995	4	4	2	5	5	..	..	..	..	..
	10–15	993	992	991	988	981	7	7	9	12	19	..	1	..	..	..
	15–20	900	959	947	939	885	96	39	52	59	111	4	2	1	2	4
	20–40	337	377	370	322	285	607	576	590	622	677	56	47	40	56	38
	40–60	35	33	36	35	32	811	814	823	818	841	154	153	141	147	127
	60 and over	20	26	21	14	25	617	637	668	679	701	363	337	311	307	274
	Females	**450**	**461**	**448**	**451**	**428**	**391**	**364**	**372**	**373**	**408**	**159**	**175**	**180**	**176**	**164**
	0–5	998	996	999	998	994	2	3	1	2	5	..	1	..	..	1
	5–10	990	992	998	995	989	9	6	2	5	10	1	2	..	..	1
	10–15	948	960	940	932	886	50	36	58	65	110	2	4	2	3	4
	15–20	448	625	606	520	376	526	353	374	449	599	26	22	20	31	25
	20–40	69	63	62	44	41	777	776	819	776	793	154	161	119	180	166
	40–60	9	10	5	9	11	420	406	383	368	381	571	584	612	623	608
	60 and over	7	12	9	8	11	128	120	94	95	109	865	868	897	897	880

ii.—Distribution by main age-periods and civil condition of 10,000 *of each sex and religion.*

Religion and age.	Males.			Females.		
	Unmarried.	Married.	Widow.	Unmarried.	Married.	Widow.
1	2	3	4	5	6	7
ALL RELIGIONS	***5,544***	***3,928***	***528***	***4,443***	***3,963***	***1,594***
0–10	2,114	5	..	2,558	15	1
10–15	1,096	7	..	1,160	68	4
15–40	2,274	2,492	212	680	3,296	568
40 and over	60	1,424	316	15	584	1,021
HINDU	***5,570***	***3,875***	***555***	***4,495***	***3,915***	***1,590***
0–10	2,195	6	..	2,610	14	2
10–15	1,117	8	..	1,171	62	3
15–40	2,198	2,455	220	700	3,257	564
40 and over.	60	1,406	335	14	582	1,021
MUSLIM	***5,284***	***4,419***	***297***	***3,784***	***4,553***	***1,663***
0–10	1,443	2	..	2,360	31	..
10–15	937	4	..	1,037	155	12
15–40	2,858	2,364	146	381	3,813	612
40 and over	46	1,549	151	6	554	1,039
CHRISTIAN	***5,667***	***3,871***	***462***	***4,233***	***4,219***	***1,548***
0–10	1,895	..	..	2,290	..	..
10–15	968	5	..	1,095	43	..
15–40	2,680	2,313	164	763	3,406	601
40 and over	124	1,553	298	85	770	947

iii.—Proportion of Sexes by civil condition at certain ages by religions.

Religion.	Number of females per 1,000 males.														
	All ages.			0–10.			10–15.			15–40.			40 and over.		
	Un.	M.	W.	Un.	M.	W.	Un.	M.	W.	Un.	M.	W.	Un.	M.	W.
1	2	3	4	5	6	7	8	9	10	11	12	13	14	15	16
All religions	644	810	2,425	983	2,277	..	851	7,470	13,000	240	1,062	2,156	204	330	2,594
Hindu	674	844	2,390	998	2,022	..	876	6,721	10,000	266	1,108	2,137	202	346	2,547
Muslim	387	557	3,023	884	7,500	..	598	18,750	..	72	720	2,260	73	194	3,719
Christian	525	765	2,355	848	..	..	995	6,000	..	200	1,034	2,576	480	348	2,233

iv.—The Distribution by civil condition of 1,000 of each sex at certain ages for selected castes.

Caste.		All ages.			0–6.			7–13.			14–16.			17–23.			24–43.			44 and over.		
		Unmarried.	Married.	Widow.	Unmarried.	Married.	Widow.	Unmarried.	Married.	Widow.	Unmarried.	Married.	Widow.	Unmarried.	Married.	Widow.	Unmarried.	Married.	Widow.	Unmarried.	Married.	Widow.
1		2	3	4	5	6	7	8	9	10	11	12	13	14	15	16	17	18	19	20	21	22
Amma Kodaga	M.	601	339	60	1,000	..	..	1,000	..	..	1,000	..	..	870	130	..	238	673	89	19	769	212
	F.	508	348	149	1,000	..	..	1,000	..	..	1,000	..	..	481	481	38	..	876	124	..	250	750
Bant	M.	578	384	38	1,000	..	..	1,000	..	..	1,000	..	..	921	79	..	392	563	45	64	807	129
	F.	429	412	159	989	11	..	949	51	..	857	143	..	296	690	14	6	784	210	33	262	705
Boya	M.	544	381	75	1,000	..	..	1,000	..	..	983	67	..	903	97	..	192	707	101	..	632	368
	F.	396	378	231	1,000	..	..	1,000	..	..	900	100	..	231	692	77	26	628	346	40	160	800
Brahman (Kanarese)	M.	549	371	80	1,000	..	..	991	9	..	1,000	..	..	824	167	9	181	739	80	28	636	336
	F.	365	372	263	1,000	..	..	955	45	..	300	700	..	8	556	436	6	585	409	..	173	827
Ganda	M.	578	375	52	1,000	..	..	994	6	..	981	17	2	872	120	8	206	738	61	25	769	206
	F.	480	385	135	998	2	..	993	6	1	911	89	..	283	705	12	14	829	157	14	303	683
Golla	M.	547	360	93	1,000	..	..	1,000	..	..	1,000	..	..	824	176	..	196	676	128	23	659	318
	F.	407	390	203	1,000	..	..	957	43	..	667	333	..	74	889	37	95	716	189	..	179	821
Holeya	M.	486	465	49	1,000	..	..	1,000	..	..	1,000	..	..	815	185	..	91	844	65	48	762	190
	F.	467	487	96	1,000	..	..	962	38	..	1,000	..	..	233	734	33	125	700	175	72	571	357
Kodaga	M.	631	323	46	1,000	..	..	998	2	..	995	5	..	919	79	2	239	703	58	22	781	197
	F.	519	340	141	998	2	..	998	2	..	971	27	2	489	500	11	22	804	174	7	356	637
Arya Vaisya (Komati)	M.	490	460	50	1,000	..	..	944	56	..	883	167	..	571	429	..	118	853	29	..	692	308
	F.	387	460	153	1,000	..	..	800	200	..	100	900	..	..	950	50	..	810	190	..	143	857
Kudiya	M.	578	359	63	1,000	..	..	1,000	..	..	1,000	..	..	788	212	..	131	762	107	29	743	228
	F.	441	380	179	1,000	..	..	956	44	..	889	111	..	270	703	27	12	776	212	..	263	738
Kuruba	M.	512	424	64	998	2	..	998	2	..	985	15	..	801	196	3	161	744	95	14	804	182
	F.	423	487	90	998	..	2	974	24	2	819	175	6	206	769	25	23	885	92	6	466	528
Labbai	M.	492	476	32	1,000	..	..	1,000	..	..	1,000	..	..	800	200	..	232	732	36	..	889	111
	F.	337	424	239	1,000	..	..	929	71	..	500	500	..	63	750	187	..	690	310	..	231	769
Lingayat	M.	603	315	82	989	11	..	995	5	..	1,000	..	..	888	108	4	293	601	106	44	688	318
	F.	402	324	274	997	3	..	989	11	..	654	332	14	93	806	101	14	564	422	5	118	877
Madiga	M.	508	459	33	1,000	..	..	1,000	..	..	1,000	..	..	500	500	..	123	816	61	..	917	83
	F.	474	368	158	1,000	..	..	1,000	..	..	250	750	..	857	643	..	..	724	276	..	223	778
Mappilla	M.	539	440	21	1,000	..	..	1,000	..	..	994	6	..	874	121	5	263	708	29	16	918	66
	F.	385	478	137	998	2	..	961	39	..	552	417	31	75	872	53	18	811	171	4	325	671
Maratha	M.	469	478	53	1,000	..	..	960	40	..	960	40	..	833	167	..	313	651	36	43	702	255
	F.	228	550	222	1,000	..	..	773	182	45	667	333	..	33	767	200	41	808	151	..	290	710
Nayar	M.	490	459	51	1,000	..	..	975	25	..	972	28	..	923	77	..	371	573	56	80	788	132
	F.	416	483	101	1,000	..	..	929	71	..	733	200	67	167	792	41	16	871	113	..	471	529
Pale	M.	466	482	52	1,000	..	..	991	9	..	986	14	..	825	172	3	194	735	71	25	818	157
	F.	361	499	140	1,000	..	..	970	24	6	623	377	..	98	840	62	20	801	179	..	229	771
Panchama	M.	514	427	59	1,000	..	..	996	4	..	976	23	1	814	179	7	183	741	76	27	749	224
	F.	408	428	164	998	2	..	996	4	..	689	290	21	163	784	53	25	740	235	3	270	727
Paraiyan	M.	478	462	60	1,000	..	..	1,000	..	..	1,000	..	..	786	179	85	118	800	82	..	800	200
	F.	359	538	103	1,000	..	..	1,000	..	..	667	333	..	143	762	95	14	873	113	..	400	600
Telaga	M.	592	381	77	1,000	..	..	1,000	..	..	875	125	..	900	100	..	200	750	50	42	583	375
	F.	406	348	246	1,000	..	..	1,000	..	..	750	250	..	250	750	..	42	646	312	..	136	864
Vakkaliga	M.	566	377	57	994	6	..	999	1	..	997	3	..	833	157	10	212	715	73	29	730	241
	F.	415	343	242	1,000	..	..	984	15	1	800	185	15	158	779	63	13	631	356	2	148	850
Yerava	M.	476	461	63	999	1	..	989	11	..	991	9	..	776	213	11	92	814	94	11	822	167
	F.	413	498	89	998	2	..	984	15	1	863	137	..	179	786	35	18	914	68	4	470	528

CHAPTER VII.

INFIRMITIES.

Reference to and value of statistics.

INSTRUCTIONS were given to the enumerators as in the previous census that all those afflicted with either insanity, deaf-mutism, blindness or leprosy should be brought on to the census record. Emphasis was laid in the instructions that to deserve an entry, insanity should be of a violent form of mental derangement, deaf-mutism should be either congenital or acquired after birth, blindness should be of both the eyes, and leprosy should be of a true character excluding cases of persons suffering from mere leucoderma or discoloration of the skin.

2. The natural reticence on the part of many afflicted with these four infirmities, particularly the loathsome disease of leprosy, to disclose or admit their existence was largely discounted by the intimate local knowledge of the enumerators.

Summary of statistics.

3. The total number of infirmities according to Imperial Table IX was 136 males and 112 females including one male suffering from double infirmity—insanity and deaf-mutism—against 66 males and 70 females in 1921. Subsidiary Table *i* shows the number afflicted per 100,000 of the population at each of the five censuses. Insanity, deaf-mutism and leprosy which were steadily on the decrease from 1891 to 1921 suddenly showed an increase in 1931, while the number of blind persons discloses a gradual rise from 1911. As compared with the figures for 1921, the number of insane persons has more than doubled itself, the figures for females showing considerable preponderance, that of deaf-mutes has increased by more than five times, the number of blind has increased only by 6 and lastly the number afflicted with leprosy has doubled. The abnormal increase in the number of deaf-mutes may be partly attributed to more births of deaf-mutes from 1921 and partly to the increased number of such imported cases among beggars, who come in larger numbers owing to the facilities provided by improved communications.

4. Subsidiary Table *ii* relates to number afflicted per 100,000 persons of each age period and number of females afflicted per 1,000 males. It is seen from the table that insanity is more common between the ages of 50–55, deaf-mutism between 15-20, blindness 60 and over, and leprosy between 50–55. Apart from this on the 1st April 1931, there were 24 persons belonging to Coorg in the Mental Hospital, Madras. The table relating to infirmities by selected castes, was abandoned under the orders of the Government of India and consequently it is not possible to state which of the communities are mostly subjected to these infirmities.

i.—Number afflicted per 100,000 *of the total population at each of the last five censuses.*

Year.	Insane.		Deaf-mute.		Blind.		Leper.		Number of females afflicted with each infirmity per 100 males.			
	Males.	Females.	Males.	Females.	Males.	Females.	Males.	Females.	Insane.	Deaf-mute.	Blind.	Leper.
1	2	3	4	5	6	7	8	9	10	11	12	13
1931 ..	14	25	61	63	64	58	12	8	138	84	72	55
1921 ..	10	8	13	11	47	69	3	7	67	67	121	167
1911 ..	11	10	42	59	47	45	6	..	73	112	76	..
1901 ..	16	20	59	56	45	63	6	4	100	76	113	50
1891 ..	26	25	80	64	49	51	13	14	76	64	83	92

ii.—Number afflicted per 100,000 *persons of each age period and number of females afflicted per* 1,000 *males.*

Age.	Number afflicted per 100,000.								Number of females afflicted per 1,000 males.			
	Insane.		Deaf-mutes.		Blind.		Leper.					
	Males.	Females.	Males.	Females.	Males.	Females.	Males.	Fameles.	Insane.	Deaf-mute	Blind.	Leper.
1	2	3	4	5	6	7	8	9	10	11	12	13
Total ..	*14*	*25*	*61*	*63*	*64*	*58*	*12*	*8*	*1,385*	*836*	*724*	*545*
0–5 ..	10	..	..	20	..	20	..	..	..	*	*	..
5–10 ..	10	11	73	66	21	22	..	..	1,000	857	1,000	..
10–15 ..	20	11	80	78	70	22	10	11	500	875	286	1,000
15–20 ..	11	27	120	67	88	40	..	13	2,000	455	375	*
20–25 ..	10	12	111	49	61	37	10	12	1,000	364	500	1,000
25–30 ..	..	42	62	84	21	56	10	..	*	1,000	2,000	..
30–35 ..	11	66	54	99	22	66	11	17	4,000	1,200	2,000	1,000
35–40 ..	14	70	28	47	42	47	28	..	3,000	1,000	667	..
40–45 ..	36	..	36	88	36	59	..	..	..	1,500	1,000	..
45–50 ..	27	40	27	120	133	120	27	40	1,000	3,000	600	1,000
50–55 ..	36	50	36	99	216	149	86	50	1,000	2,000	500	1,000
55–60 ..	61	..	61	..	306	210	61	..	..	..	600	..
60 and over	..	41	..	..	399	372	80	..	*	..	900	..

* The strict mathematical figure is infinity (∞). With such small totals proportional figures are really worthless.

CHAPTER VIII.

OCCUPATION.

Reference to statistics. Of all the subjects dealt with at a census, that of occupations is decidedly the most intricate and difficult. The difficulty is, however, minimised to a very considerable extent in Coorg, owing to the absence of organized industries of any kind conducted on large scales. The All-India industrial tables have been dispensed with and Imperial Table X relating to occupation has been prepared from the information gathered in columns 9–12 of the census questionnaire. Column 9 was required to show whether a person was an earner or dependent. One who made a regular individual contribution to the family income was considered to be an earner. The next column was reserved only for 'earners' shown in column 9 and in it, the principal occupation of the earner was ordered to be entered. The occupation normally and regularly followed and which produced the major portion of the income constituted the principal occupation. Column 11 served a twofold purpose as it showed not only a subsidiary occupation pursued by an earner in addition to his principal occupation which brought him the next best income but also the occupation followed by a person, shown as dependent in column 9, though he was really a working dependent having no principal occupation. No entry relating to a working dependent was made in column 11 unless he had contributed to the support of the household. A house-wife who regularly managed the kitchen by manual labour was considered to be a working dependent. Column 12 was specially meant for organized workers. Imperial Table XI, relating to occupations of selected communities was not, however, compiled for Coorg. An analysis of the figures in the Imperial Table X are found in the two subsidiary tables appended at the end of this chapter.

Accuracy of the statistics. 2. The occupations returned in the general schedule represent the economic position of the people on the census day. In an agricultural country like Coorg, a very large number of people, who are agriculturists, will be engaged in cultivation for only a certain period of the year and during the rest of the year pursue other occupations such as unskilled day labourers, petty contractors etc. The classification of the subsidiary occupation is generally difficult, but errors in this direction are few and negligible as far as Coorg is concerned. Caste and occupation are often confused and the traditional instead of actual occupation is sometimes noted. But such mistakes have been avoided by proper instructions to enumerators and supervision over their work. Errors due to the use of such vague words as 'service', 'clerk', 'contractor', 'labourer', etc., have been completely avoided. Special instructions in vernacular were given to distinguish between 'earner', 'working dependent' and 'non-working dependent' and principal and subsidiary occupations and also to fill up occupations in respect of cultivators of different kinds. It is possible that some of the working dependents might have been shown as 'earners' and *vice versa*, and some inaccuracy might have crept in as regards females. It is also possible that there might be a few errors in distinguishing the different kinds of cultivators. Subject to the above exceptions, the occupation statistics may be considered to be fairly accurate. The classification was done in the abstraction office at Mangalore.

Basis of the returns. 3. To have a clear idea of the basis of returns, it is essential to examine some of the distinctive features of the occupation census of 1931. Certain changes have been introduced into the general schedule, as a result of which any useful comparison with the figures of the previous censuses, is not feasible. While the total population pursuing each avocation was shown in 1921, only the distribution of workers (earners and working dependents) has now been shown, with the result that the apportionment of the dependents among the different occupations has been dispensed with. Another notable and useful alteration is that in the place of 'workers' and 'dependents' of 1921, a three-fold division of 'earner', 'working dependent' and 'non-working dependent' has been introduced.

4. Apart from these changes in the schedule itself a few alterations in the occupational classification mostly in the nature of amplification, has been introduced. Notable among them are (1) occupations against group 3 of 1921 were subdivided into three separate groups of 2, 3 and 4 : but there are no entries against these items in respect of Coorg. (2) Another useful expansion was that group 7 of 1921 was subdivided into groups 9–16, showing different plantation products. (3) Old groups, 26–27, 52–54, 60–64, 66–70 and 85–89 have been combined into single groups of 43, 65, 70, 81 and 90 respectively. Similarly, old groups 31–35 have been re-arranged in groups 46 and 47. (4) Persons under group 101—order 18—in last census, have been shifted to group 183 in order 49 ; and witches and wizards have been transferred from sub-class XII—Unproductive—to sub-class VIII—Profession and Literal Art (group 181), etc. In fine the changes have resulted in the groups of occupation rising from 191 to 195 during the decade.

Summary of statistics.

5. The figures of 'earners', 'working dependents' and 'non-working dependents' are 84,573, 27,100 and 51,654 respectively. The number of dependents at the last census was 62,793, which is 11,139 more than the figure for 1931. The number of persons aged below 10, who are usually dependents, in 1931 was 38,138 as against 39,478 in 1921. The only explanation for the abnormal decrease in the number of dependents is that many of the females doing regular cooking work, who might have been shown as dependents in 1921 have now been shown as working dependents.

Production of raw materials.

6. The province, as every other part of India, is mainly agricultural. Information in class A—Production of raw materials—in the Imperial Table is therefore of great importance to Coorg. Out of 125,228 persons, following some occupation or other, 62,631 or 50 per cent are engaged in the production of raw materials. Viewed from another point, out of 111,673 'workers' and 'working dependents', 60,816 or over 54 per cent are living by production of raw materials. The percentage of agriculturists comes to nearly 72 of the actual earners. That the province is pre-eminently agricultural is all the more vivid if 25,000 female working dependents mainly engaged in domestic service are excluded when considering the proportions of agriculturists to total earners and working dependents.

7. Turning to details, it is seen that non-cultivating proprietors have increased from 718 to 2,186 during the decade, but cultivating owners have decreased from 24, 791 males to 21,671 and 18,280 females to 3,714. The change can only be attributed to more correct enumeration. The explanation for the great drop in female cultivators is that many females, who mainly did cooking work, and occasionally assisted the males in the fields must have been classified as cultivators at the last census and as working dependents under domestic service in 1931. Similarly, the figures for tenant cultivators also show a decline. Persons engaged in the cultivation of special crops show an increase from 11,983 to 13,156. The details under different crops are given in Imperial Table X. The decrease in the number of persons engaged in 'Forestry' from 1,703 to 251 is attributed to the closing of the 'sawmills' and the Makut tramway works, owing to their unproductive nature.

Preparation and supply of material substances.

8. Coming to class B of the table, there is practically no organized industry in Coorg, established even on a fairly large scale. The only organized industries on a small scale are the tea factory at Glen Lorna near Hudikeri in South Coorg, and the two rice mills in North and South Coorg. The Agave cultivation in Fraserpet and all the rubber plantations have been closed temporarily, owing to the heavy fall in prices of these products. Details as regards the other minor industries, which have not in any way expanded, are given in the table.

Public Administration and Liberal Arts.

9. Under class C—Public Administration and Liberal Arts—the total number of persons following occupations is 2,105 against 2,336 in 1921. The reduction is mainly due to retrenchment of staff.

Miscellaneous.

10. The increase under class D—Miscellaneous—is due to the inclusion as working dependents of 25,000 females who were only assisting the family with domestic service.

i. a.—General distribution of occupation and principal occupation of females [Earners (principal occupation) and Working Dependents.]

Class, sub-class and order.	Number per 10,000 of total population.	Number of females per 1,000 males.
1	2	3
Non-working dependents ..	3,163	..
All occupations ..	6,837	..
[Earners (principal occupation) and working dependents.]		
A. Production of raw materials ..	3,723	354
I. Exploitation of animals and vegetation	3,723	354
1. Pasture and agriculture ..	3,720	354
(a) Cultivation ..	2,876	318
(b) Cultivation of special crops, fruit, etc. (planters, manager, clerks and labourers).	791	..
(c) Forestry ..	15	4
(d) Stock raising ..	38	30
(e) Raising of small animals and insects	..	..
2. Fishing and hunting ..	8	815
II. Exploitation of minerals—		
3. Metallic minerals ..	..	..
4. Non-metallic minerals ..	..	..
B. Preparation and supply of material substances	515	130
III. Industry ..	237	201
5. Textiles ..	4	148
6. Hides, skins and hard materials from the animal kingdom	..	..
7. Wood ..	51	221
8. Metals ..	13	14
9. Ceramics ..	16	962
10. Chemical products properly so-called and analogous	1	..
11. Food Industries ..	42	96
12. Industries of dress and the toilet ..	62	311
13. Furniture industries ..	..	..
14. Building industries ..	16	92
15. Construction of means of transport	5	..
16. Production and transmission of physical force	..	..
17. Miscellaneous and undefined industries	27	85
IV. Transport ..	94	9
18. Transport by air ..	..	..
19. Transport by water ..	..	..
20. Transport by road ..	90	5
21. Transport by rail ..	1	..
22. Post office, Telegraph and Telephone services	3	109
V. Trade ..	184	115
23. Banks, establishments of credit, exchange and insurance	1	67
24. Brokerage commission and export	6	24
25. Trade in textiles ..	11	6
26. Trade in skins, leather and furs ..	1	..
27. Trade in wood ..	..	200
28. Trade in metals ..	2	31
29. Trade in pottery, bricks and tiles ..	..	..
30. Trade in chemical products ..	..	..
31. Hotels, cafés, restaurants, etc. ..	19	109
32. Other trade in foodstuffs ..	108	129
33. Trade in clothing and toilet articles	..	..
34. Trade in furniture ..	1	267
35. Trade in building materials ..	..	1,000
36. Trade in means of transport ..	1	..
37. Trade in fuel ..	..	..
38. Trade in articles of luxury and those pertaining to letters and the arts and sciences.	6	429
39. Trade of other sorts ..	28	87
C. Public Administration and Liberal Arts	90	76
VI. Public Force ..	11	..
40. Army ..	..	..
41. Navy ..	..	..
42. Air Force ..	..	..
43. Police ..	11	..
VII. Public Administration ..	22	9
44. Public Administration ..	22	9
VIII. Professional and Literal Arts ..	57	121
45. Religion ..	20	63
46. Law ..	2	..
47. Medicine ..	9	171
48. Instruction ..	21	148
49. Letters, arts and sicences (other than 44)	5	200
Miscellaneous ..	2,509	2,935
IX. Persons living on their income ..	2	118
50. Persons living principally on their income	2	118
X. Domestic service ..	1,698	1,1847
51. Domestic service ..	1,698	11,847
XI. Insufficiently described occupations ..	797	612
52. General terms which do not indicate a definite occupation	797	612
XII. Unproductive ..	12	367
53. Inmates of jails, asylums and almshouses	..	..
54. Beggars, vagrants, prostitutes ..	12	367
55. Other unclassified, non-productive industries	..	..

i. b.—General distribution of occupation (Earners as subsidiary occupation).

Class, sub-class and order.	Number per 10,000 of total population.
1	2
All occupations (Earners as subsidiary occupation.)	830
A. Production of raw materials	111
I. Exploitation of animals and vegetation—	111
1. Pasture and agriculture	111
(a) Cultivation	91
(b) Cultivation of special crops, fruit, etc. (planters, managers, clerks and labourers)	15
(c) Forestry	4
(d) Stock-raising	1
(e) Raising of small animals and insects	..
2. Fishing and hunting	..
II. Exploitation of minerals—	
3. Metallic minerals	..
4. Non-metallic minerals	..
B. Preparation and supply of material substances	169
III. Industry	69
5. Textiles	..
6. Hides, skins and hard materials from the animal kingdom	..
7. Wood	20
8. Metals	6
9. Ceramics	4
10. Chemical products properly so-called and analogous	1
11. Food industries	8
12. Industries of dress and the toilet	21
13. Furniture industries	..
14. Building industries	3
15. Construction of means of transport	..
16. Production and transmission of physical force	..
17. Miscellaneous and undefined industries	6
IV. Transport	55
18. Transport by air	..
19. Transport by water	..
20. Transport by road	53
21. Transport by rail	..
22. Post office, Telegraph and Telephone services	2
V. Trade	45
23. Banks, establishments of credit, exchange and insurance	7
24. Brokerage commission and export	2
25. Trade in textiles	2
26. Trade in skins, leather and furs.	..
27. Trade in wood	1
28. Trade in metals	1
29. Trade in pottery, bricks and tiles	..
30. Trade in chemical products	..
31. Hotels, cafés, restaurants, etc.	2
32. Other trade in foodstuffs	22
33. Trade in clothing and toilet articles	..
34. Trade in furniture	1
35. Trade in building materials	..
36. Trade in means of transport.	..
37. Trade in fuel	..
38. Trade in articles of luxury and those pertaining to letters and the arts and sciences	2
39. Trade of other sorts	5
C. Public Administration and Liberal Arts.	39
VI. Public Force	1
40. Army	..
41. Navy	..
42. Air Force	..
43. Police	1
VII. Public Administration	19
44. Public Administration	19
VIII. Professional and Literal Arts	19
45. Religion	8
46. Law	..
47 Medicine	1
48. Instruction	4
49. Letters, arts and sciences (other than 44)	6
D. Miscellaneous	511
IX. Persons living on their income	4
50. Persons living principally on their income	4
X. Domestic service	491
51. Domestic service	491
XI. Insufficiently described occupations	15
52. General terms which do not indicate a definite occupation.	15
XII. Unpoductive	1
53. Inmates of jails, asylums and almshouses	..
54. Beggars, vagrants, prostitutes.	1
55. Other unclassified non-productive industries	..

ii-a.—Distribution by sub-classes of the occupations of earners' (principal occupations) and working dependents in the Province.

Province.	Total 1,000.			Number per mille of the total population occupied as earners (principal occupation) and working dependents in											
	Non-working dependents.	Working dependents.	Earner (principal occupation).	Sub-class I. Exploitation of animals and vegetation.	Sub-class II. Exploitation of minerals.	Sub-class III. Industry.	Sub-class IV. Transport.	Sub-class V. Trade.	Sub-class VI. Public Force.	Sub-class VII. Public Administration.	Sub-class VIII. Professions and Liberal Arts.	Sub-class IX. Persons living on their income.	Sub-class X. Domestic service.	Sub-class XI. Insufficiently described occupation.	Sub-class XII. Unproductive.
1	2	3	4	5	6	7	8	9	10	11	12	13	14	15	16
Coorg	316·3	165·9	517·8	372·4	..	23·7	9·4	18·4	11	2·2	5·7	0·2	169·7	79·7	1·2

ii-b.—Distribution by sub-classes of subsidiary occupation in the Province.

Province.	Number per mille of the total population of earners having a subsidiary occupation in											
	Sub-class I.	Sub-class II.	Sub-class III.	Sub-class IV.	Sub-class V.	Sub-class VI.	Sub-class VII.	Sub-class VIII.	Sub-class IX.	Sub-class X.	Sub-class XI.	Sub-class XII.
1	2	3	4	5	6	7	8	9	10	11	12	13
Coorg	11·1	..	6·9	5·5	4·5	0·1	1·9	1·9	0·4	49·0	1·5	0·1

CHAPTER IX.

LITERACY.

Nature of returns.

THE standard prescribed at the last census that a person was to be described as literate, if he could write a letter to a friend and read the answer to it, has been retained at the present census. The enumerators had clear instructions on this point and the statistics may be regarded as approximately accurate. Instructions were also issued as at the last census to show literacy in English in a separate column. The number of literates who had completed their primary education was recorded in the schedules but the figures obtained were not compiled in the abstraction office.

Reference to statistics.

2. Imperial Table XIII gives particulars of literacy by religion and age and Imperial Table XIV deals with the number of literate males and females of each caste, tribe or race. At the end of this chapter are appended five subsidiary tables showing the following statistical particulars :—

(i) (*a*) literacy by age, sex and religion,

(*b*) education of Christians by race,

(ii) English literacy by age, sex and religion,

(iii) progress of literacy since 1891,

(iv) literacy by caste, and

(v) the number of institutions and pupils according to the return of the Educational department.

Summary of the statistics.

3. During the past decade, the number of literates in the province increased from 20,643 to 25,336 or by 23 per cent. If the sex figures are taken into consideration, it is interesting to note that while the male literates have only increased by 2,933 or 17 per cent, the female literates have increased by 1,760 or 48 per cent. The floating population of nearly 38,000, which comprises mostly illiterates and also the decrease of 511 in the total population should be borne in mind while appraising the figures of increase under 'literates'. The vast progress in female education made during the decade is noteworthy. The figures tabulated below disclose the position of Coorg in literacy in comparison with some of the provinces and states in India :—

Provinces or States.	Population of literates per 1,000 aged 5 and over.			Provinces or States.	Population of literates per 1,000 aged 5 and over.		
	Persons.	Males.	Females.		Persons.	Males.	Females.
Burma	367	560	164	Bengal	110	180	32
Cochin	337	460	220	Madras	108	187	30
Travancore ..	288	408	168	Bombay	108	174	32
Coorg	176	246	87	Mysore	106	174	33
Delhi	163	226	72	Hyderabad ..	47	78	11

Coorg stands fourth, Burma, Cochin and Travancore taking the first three places. Though comparison of statistics relating to Coorg with other provinces and states, so vastly varying in area, population, climate and resources serves no useful purpose, yet it indicates that Coorg is not very backward in education and that there has been steady progress from decade to decade. The percentage of literates in English to that of the total population is nearly 3 and to that of total literates 16, taking only those over 5 years into consideration.

Literacy by taluks.

Provincial Table II shows the Talukwar figures of literacy. It is seen that in North Coorg there are 8,523 males and 1,930 females and in South Coorg, 11,369 males and 3,514 females literate in vernaculars, which means that 20 per cent of the male population and 5 per cent of the female population in North Coorg are literate while the percentages for South Coorg are 24 for males and 8 for females. Turning to literacy in English, 3·5 per cent of males and 1·2 per cent of females in North Coorg are literate, the corresponding percentages for South Coorg being 3·7 for males and 0·7 for females. The Coorgs who are predominant in every walk of life evince keen interest in education, both in vernacular and English and as they are mostly in South Coorg, literacy figures for that taluk are comparatively superior. The proportion has, however, greatly diminished as most of the educated persons of the taluk are in Government service working at the headquarters of the province, Mercara, which is situated in North Coorg. The preponderance of female literates in English in North Coorg is mainly attributed to the presence of many literate women in Mercara, mostly belonging to South Coorg who are the wives and children of well-to-do Coorgs and Government servants. The existence of the Girls' High School is another contributory factor to the larger number of English literates among females in North Coorg.

4. The progress in education among the main religions in the province from 1901, is illustrated below :— **Literacy by religion.**

Religion.	Number per 10,000 of all ages, who are literate.							
	1931.		1921.		1911.		1901.	
	Males.	Females.	Males.	Females.	Males.	Females.	Males.	Females.
All Religions ..	2,196	748	1,895	496	1,570	279	1,277	157
Hindus	2,186	756	2,146	560	1,688	288	1,206	126
Muslims	1,885	275	1,894	210	1,834	160	1,687	126
Christians	3,886	1,894	3,508	2,036	3,605	1,940	3,522	1,693

5. The Christians as before are in the forefront, though for the first time since 1901, the female literates show a fall. Subsidiary Table *i-a* deals with the education of Christians by race. Among Muslims, it may be noted, that while the figures for females since 1901 have more than doubled themselves, those for males have remained almost stationary, except for a slight increase during 1901–1911. Turning to Hindus, the female figures since 1901 have increased by six times, while those for males have almost doubled themselves. If Brahmans and depressed classes are excluded from Hindus, 20,736 literates are found for a population of 117,941 or 18 per cent. Further, if forest tribes who number 19,677 are excluded, the percentage of literates works out to 21.

6. Taking all religions into consideration, a steady and marked progress in education is clearly visible. This is evident from the fact that while there were 76 public institutions and 4,156 scholars receiving education therein in 1901, there were in 1931, 111 public institutions and 9,964 scholars. (Subsidiary Table *v*.)

7. The undermentioned table below compares the figures for literacy in the three main age periods above 10 years among the chief religions since 1901. In all the three age-groups, a continuous and steady growth of literates is seen, among all religions and Hindus. Similar progress is also noticed among Muslims and Christians but the curve of progress takes an undulating course. Literates in the age-group 15-20 furnish a good guide to the number of children who have been under effective instruction during the preceding quinquennium. A comparison of the number returned as literate at this age-period during each succeeding census indicates that from decade to decade, for every religion except Christianity, steady progress is made, among both the sexes. The progress of female education among Hindus is appreciable, being over four times the figures for 1901. Among Christians, though there is improvement, when compared with the figures for 1901, there was a decrease among male literates during 1911–21, and among female literates during 1921–31. The reason is that a portion of Christians are immigrants, and the figures of literacy fluctuate with the number of literates among the immigrants. Considering persons aged 5 years and over, the percentage of literates among males, to that of the male population works out to 25, the corresponding percentage for females being 9. In Madras, the similar percentage for males is 19 and for females 3. **Literacy by age.**

Literate in both sexes.

Religion.	10–15								15–20			
	1931.		1921.		1911.		1901.		1931.		1921.	
	M.	F.	M.	F.	M.	F.	M.	F.	M.	F.	M.	F.
1	2	3	4	5	6	7	8	9	10	11	12	13
All Religions	1,777	845	1,416	652	1,096	361	1,098	243	2,499	1,028	1,881	792
Hindus	1,626	790	1,271	603	995	304	839	191	2210	970	1,669	737
Muslims	89	18	96	13	65	16	81	7	204	22	146	18
Christians	60	33	43	36	35	36	65	42	83	32	49	34

Religion.	15–20.				20 and over.							
	1911.		1901.		1931.		1921.		1911.		1901.	
	M.	F.	M.	F.	M.	F.	M.	F.	M.	F.	M.	F.
	14	15	16	17	18	19	20	21	22	23	24	25
All Religions	1,691	466	1,578	284	14,591	3,065	13,360	2,047	12,317	1,252	9,974	675
Hindus	1,451	397	1,373	235	12,619	2,978	11,440	1,769	10,370	990	8,160	447
Muslims	155	13	136	12	1,350	79	1,319	61	1,316	46	1,204	43
Christians	82	51	61	36	601	180	485	208	586	207	579	180

Literacy in English.

8. Literacy in English education is dealt with in Subsidiary Table *iv* and also in the last three columns of Imperial Tables VIII and IX. The remarkable enthusiasm for English education evinced during 1911–21, was kept up during the last decade ; the number of such literates being 362 per 10,000 in the case of males and 97 in the case of females, against 141 and 24, respectively in 1901. The Muhammadans are still averse to English education and more particularly so their females, among whom 2 literates for 10,000 population are recorded. The Christians are naturally more advanced in English education, though female literates among them during the past decade decreased from 945 to 728 per 10,000 of population. The percentage of literates in English among those aged 5 and over to that of the total persons aged 5 and over, in each sex comes to 4 for males and 1 for females. Similar percentages in Madras are 3 for males and 0·3 for females.

Literacy among various castes and tribes.

9. Imperial Table XIV and Subsidiary Table *v* deal with literacy by caste. Of all the communities, the most advanced in literacy are the Brahmans, among whom there are 744 literates including 246 literates in English, for a population of 1,203 persons, aged 7 years and over. The progress of education among Coorgs is maintained. There are 13,184 literates including 2,400 literates in English out of 33,753 persons aged 7 years and over. The proportion of female literates in English among Coorgs, however, is higher than among Brahmans. The Gauda and Lingayat communities come next to Coorgs with 2,115 and 725 literates for 11,579 and 4,400 persons, aged 7 years and over, respectively. Among Adi-Dravidas, Balagai, Holeya, Madiga and Panchama aged 7 and over, there were 233 males and 42 females literate and 6 males literate in English. There has been hardly any improvement in literacy among these classes and this is attributed to the unwillingness on the part of parents to send their children to schools, in spite of the several inducements offered to them. There were in 1931–32 five Panchama schools against twelve in 1921–22. The Yeravas are in no way better as there are only 15 males and 8 females literate for a population of 5,539 males and 4,826 females aged 7 years and over. A special Yerava school opened in 1925 had to be closed for want of sufficient attendance.

i.—Literacy by age, sex and religion.

Religion.	Number per 10,000 who are literate. All ages. Total.	M.	F.	0–10. M.	F.	10–15. M.	F.	15–20. M.	F.	20 and over. M.	F.	Number per 10,000 who are illiterate. Total.	Males.	Females.	Number per 10,000 above who are literate in English. Total.	Males.	Females.
1	2	3	4	5	6	7	8	9	10	11	12	13	14	15	16	17	18
All religions ..	1,551	2,196	748	534	267	1,778	943	2,737	1,369	2,792	821	8,449	7,804	9,252	244	362	97
Hindu	1,535	2,186	756	537	267	1,817	962	2,817	1,424	2,788	823	8,465	7,814	9,245	232	352	89
Muslims ..	1,320	1,885	275	333	121	1,057	309	1,899	402	2,354	310	8,680	8,115	9,725	84	130	2
Christians ..	3,064	3,886	1,894	1,021	710	3,061	2,050	4,049	2,192	4,878	2,296	6,936	6,114	8,106	1,329	1,752	728

i-a.—Education of Christians by race.

Race.	Number per 10,000. Males. Literates.	Literates in English.	Females. Literates.	Literates in English.
1	2	3	4	5
European and allied races	8,356	8,356	7,925	7,925
Anglo-Indians	5,909	5,909	7,500	7,500
Indian .. Roman Catholics	2,889	1,079	965	189
Indian .. Syrians	5,000	2,857	5,000	..
Indian .. Others	8,021	3,165	3,734	442

ii.—English Literacy by age, sex and religion.

Religion.	Number per 10,000 who are literate in English. All ages. Total.	M.	F.	0–10. M.	F.	10–15. M.	F.	15–20. M.	F.	20 and over. M.	F.	1921. M.	F.	1911. M.	F.	1901. M.	F.
1	2	3	4	5	6	7	8	9	10	11	12	13	14	15	16	17	18
All religions ..	244	362	97	52	32	266	135	574	218	457	96	267	56	169	31	141	24
Hindu	232	352	89	50	32	274	135	597	216	442	82	299	47	167	15	116	4
Muslim	84	130	2	23	..	71	..	168	..	155	4	95	11	44	..	81	..
Christian ..	1,329	1,752	728	209	93	714	559	1,805	1,096	2,386	957	1,575	945	1,571	913	1,778	990

iii.—Progress of Literacy since 1891.

Province.	All ages 10 and over literate per 10,000. Males. 1931.	1921.	1911.	1901.	1891.	Females. 1931.	1921.	1911.	1901.	1891.
1	2	3	4	5	6	7	8	9	10	11
Coorg	2,643	2,378	1,936	1,592	1,769	918	643	357	203	162

Province.	15–20—literate per 10,000. Males. 1931.	1921.	1911.	1901.	Females. 1931.	1921.	1911.	1901.	20 and over—literate per 10,000. Males. 1931.	1921.	1911.	1901.	Females. 1931.	1921.	1911.	1901.
	12	13	14	15	16	17	18	19	20	21	22	23	24	25	26	27
Coorg	2,737	2,258	1,670	1,620	1,369	1,205	570	367	2,792	2,560	2,137	1,725	821	523	305	164

iv.—Literacy by caste.

Caste.	Number per 1,000 who are literate.				Number per 10,000 who are literate in English.			
	1931.		1921.		1931.		1921.	
	Males.	Females.	Males.	Females.	Males.	Females.	Males.	Females.
1	2	3	4	5	6	7	8	9
Gauda	*302 †254	44 36	293	54	248 208	7 6	129	27
Holeya	12 11	.. ..	23	1	62 54	.. ..	7	..
Kodaga	550 452	228 188	305	101	1,108 912	305 251	612	70
Kuruba	7 6	2 1	3	2	3 3	5 ..	..	..
Lingayat	330 289	31 27	212	22	417 364	82 71	90	68
Maratha	108 106	77 72	73	11	199 194	.. ..	18	..
Mappilla	172 159	25 21	141	11	36 33	30 25	8	..
Pale	4 4	.. ..	31	2	.. ..	.. ..	..	..
Vakkaliga	147 129	14 12	74	5	57 50	3 3	57	..
Yerava	3 2	2 1	2	1	.. ..	8 7	..	..

* The figure in the top under each caste gives the proportion excluding persons aged 0–6.
† The figure at the bottom gives the proportion on the total population.

v.—Number of Institutions and Pupils according to the return of the Educational Department.

Class of Institutions.	1931. Number of		1921. Number of		1911. Number of		1901. Number of		1891. Number of	
	Institutions.	Scholars.	Institutions.	Scholars.	Institutions.	Scholars.	Institutions.	Scholars.	Institutions.	Scholars.
1	2	3	4	5	6	7	8	9	10	11
Public.										
Secondary Schools—										
(a) Upper Secondary ..	3	1,056	2	681	1	228	1	258	2	307
(b) Lower Secondary ..	..	..	1	139	2	218	1	272	1	160
Primary Schools— (a) Upper Primary .. (b) Lower Primary ..	* 108	8,908	109	7,491	87	5,442	73	3,613	71	3,859
Training Schools ..	..	..	1	36	1	22	1	13	1	12
Private.										
Advanced Elementary— Other schools not conforming to departmental standards ..	17	405	5	78	38	780	25	567	35	457

* Includes one Industrial School.

CHAPTER X.

LANGUAGE.

Reference to statistics. THE statistics relating to linguistic distribution of the people are presented in parts I and II of Imperial Table XV. The subsidiary table appended at the end of this chapter gives the distribution of the total population by language according to the Linguistic Survey of India. The data were collected from information furnished in columns 14 and 15 of the census questionnaire.

Accuracy of returns. 2. Prior to 1931, the existence of bi-lingualism used to give some discretion to the enumerators in selecting the language, which each person ordinarily used in his own house and consequently the accuracy of the language returns was open to doubt according to the extent of bi-lingualism. To overcome this defect a new column for subsidiary languages was opened in 1931 and this arrangement had the desired effect of minimising indiscriminate entries relating to the mother-tongue spoken. The new information about subsidiary languages is compiled in part II of Imperial Table XV and forms a special feature of the language census of this year. The language first spoken from the cradle was considered to be the mother-tongue, and the language or languages habitually spoken in addition to the mother-tongue in one's daily life was entered as subsidiary.

Distribution of population by language. 3. The principal indigenous languages of the province are 'Kodagu' and 'Yerava'. The other languages spoken are, Kanarese, Malayalam, Tulu, Hindustani, Tamil, Telugu, Kurumba, Konkani, Marati and Gujarati. There are, however, separate figures relating to persons talking Arabic and European languages. At the 1931 census, 44,585 persons have been returned as speaking 'Kodagu' as their mother-tongue against 39,681 and 42,784 persons in 1921 and 1911 respectively. The population of Coorgs by caste is 41,026. Taking into consideration the fact that many other minor communities such as, Heggade, Golla, Kembattis, etc., speak 'Kodagu' as their mother-tongue, the language figures for 'Kodagu' can be accepted as accurate. As regards the Yerava language, it is to be noted that while the actual Yerava population is 12,810, persons who have been returned as speaking Yerava language as their mother-tongue number only 10,026. It is common knowledge that a Yerava, with whatever languages he may be conversant and however civilized he may be, will not forget his mother-tongue and will only speak his mother-tongue in his home. It thus seems to be fairly clear that either the language figures or the population figures of Yeravas are somewhat inaccurate.

Dravidian languages. 4. Among the dravidian group, there are five languages and two dialects, excluding the Kodagu language and Yerava dialect. Of these, Tamil, Malayalam, Tulu and Telugu speaking persons show an increase over the figures of 1921 while Kanarese speaking persons show a decrease of nearly 7,000. These languages are spoken mostly by immigrants, and consequently fluctuations in their number *ipso facto* result in variations in the number speaking different languages. The Kanarese language is, however, spoken by an overwhelming majority of 62,769. The number conversant with 'Kuruba' dialect discloses considerable diminution from 3,737 to 2,394 ; this is due to the decrease in their population. Among the other languages spoken, Marati shows a 50 per cent increase while Hindustani shows a decline of nearly 30 per cent.

Foreign Languages. 5. The number of persons speaking the English language shows a decrease of 8 (254 against 262 in 1921), while the total number of Europeans and Anglo-Indians is 222. There is a continuous decrease since 1911, in the number of persons speaking English. The number speaking Arabic and Portuguese shows a slight increase.

Distribution of Total Population by language according to linguistic survey.

Family, sub-family, branch and sub-branch.	Group.	Language.	Dialect.	Number of speakers. 1931.	1921.	1911.	Number per 10,000 of population of Province (1931).
1	2	3	4	5	6	7	8
			Grand total.	***163,327***	***163,838***	***174,976***	
I.—Languages of India.							
Dravidian family	Dravida group	Tamil	..	3,007	2,062	4,291	184
			Korava	6	3	..	..
		Malayalam	..	14,914	10,915	13,909	913
			Yerava	10,026	13,686	14,916	614
		Kanarese	..	62,769	69,431	67,545	3,844
			Kurumba	2,394	3,737	4,012	147
		Kodagu or Coorgi	..	44,585	39,681	42,784	2,730
		Tulu	..	14,275	13,145	14,226	874
		Andhra language—Telugu	..	2,668	1,082	2,688	163
			Total	***154,644***	***153,742***	***164,371***	..
Indo-European family. Aryan sub-family. Indo-Aryan Branch Outer sub-branch.	Southern group	Marathi	..	1,577	1,031	1,741	97
			Konkani	2,331	2,514	2,696	143
			Others	..	..	11	..
Inner sub-branch	Central group	Western Hindi	Hindustani	4,378	6,194	5,527	268
		Gujarati	..	53	26	129	3
		Rajasthani	Lambadi	7	25	60	..
			Others	8	..	9	..
			Total	***8,354***	***9,790***	***10,173***	..
II.—Languages Foreign to India.							
Semitic family	..	Arabic	..	19	7	6	1
Indo-European family.	Romance	Portuguese	..	50	37	67	3
	Teutonic	English	..	254	262	345	16
			Others	6	..	10	..
			Total	***329***	***306***	***428***	..
		Others	..	..	..	4	..

CHAPTER XI.

RELIGION.

THIS chapter deals with the figures in Imperial Table XVI relating to distribution of population by religion and Provincial Table II concerning population of districts and taluks by religion. The main features of the statistics relating to religion are set out in the three subsidiary tables appended at the end of this chapter which show (i) the general distribution of the population by religion, (ii) the number and variation of Christian population and (iii) the religion of the urban and rural population. **Reference to statistics.**

2. The enumerators were instructed to enter in column 4 of the schedule the religion as given out by each individual without cavil, viz., Hindu, Muslim, Christian, Sikh, Jain or Parsi and they were also instructed to enter the sect after the general name. The variations in the number following Hinduism, Christianity and Muhammadanism are dealt with separately below. The number of Jains shows a substantial decrease during the decade—83 against 202 in 1921. They are a dwindling sect in Coorg, and their main connections being with Mysore Jains, most of them have alienated their landed interest here and migrated into Mysore Province. The position of Buddhists is in no way better and they have gone down from 14 to 3 during the decade. The figures for Parsis are 12 males and 15 females. **Variation by religion.**

3. The term 'Hinduism' cannot be defined appropriately. A common and vague definition is that all persons who recognize caste, who worship orthodox deities, the incarnations of Vishnu or Shiva, their wives or their offsprings, divine mothers, spirits of trees, rocks and streams, etc., and who are governed by any system of Hindu Law, are Hindus. The term is so elastic that it includes every Indian who owns no allegiance to any other definite creed. This is particularly so in the case of Coorg since every one who is not a Muslim, Christian, Jain, Buddhist, Parsi and Agnostic, is classed as a Hindu. The total number of persons returned as Hindu in 1931 is 146,007 which is 89 per cent of the total population, the corresponding figures for 1921 being 126,697 and 77 per cent. The difference of nearly 20,000 is due to the classification of certain forest tribes as Hindus who were enumerated as animists in 1921. 'Brahmos' and 'Aryas' are not found in Coorg. The one Brahmo, who has been returned in 1931 is presumably an outsider. **Hinduism.**

4. The figures for this religion show an increase from 13,021 to 13,777 which is certainly not due to conversions or re-conversions but partly to the increased number of immigrants for purposes of trade and work in the plantations as labourers and partly to a slight increase in the indigenous population. **Muhammadanism.**

5. The number and variations in the Christian religion from 1881 is clearly indicated in Subsidiary Table *ii*. Having risen gradually till 1901, the population showed a decrease in the following two censuses of 1911 and 1921. The 1931 census, however, recorded an increase from 3,182 to 3,425. Owing to the non-compilation of Imperial Table XI relating to distribution of Christian population by sect and race, it is not possible to compare the figures for the different sects. However, Roman Catholics have increased from 2,778 to 2,808 and the Indian Christian population from 2,979 to 3,208 during the decade. The increase may be due to influx of coolies and maistris. Proselytism, however, does not evince any progress in Coorg. **Christianity.**

Reference to statistics.

6. The apparent inconsistency between the Christian figures in Imperial Table XVI and those in Imperial Tables VII, XIII and Provincial Table II, represents five Europeans, who returned their religion as Agnostic; they were considered as 'others'. for the purpose of Imperial Table XVI, but included among Christians for other tables.

Urban and rural population.

7. The distribution of urban and rural population by religion in proportions of 10,000, is dealt with in Subsidiary Table *iii.* Hindus who had gained in the urban area and lost in the rural area in 1921, have again gained in the urban area. But in the rural area, though according to the table, there is a very substantial increase from 7,810 to 9,092 per 10,000 of population, this growth is more apparent than real as all the forest tribes classed as animists in 1921, were treated as Hindus in 1931. In the case of Muslims, they have again gained in the rural area. Their loss in urban areas is only nominal, as the lower proportion is brought about by the increase of nearly 1,000 in the total urban population. Numerically they have gained by 153 in the two towns. Christians have gained in the rural area, and as in the case of Muslims, their loss in the urban area is only nominal. Numerically, they too have gained by 9.

i.—General Distribution of the Population by religion.

Religion.	Actual number in 1931.	Proportion per 10,000 of population in 1931.	1921.	1911.	1901.	1891.	1881.	Variation in per cent, increase + : Decrease —. 1921–1931.	1911–1921.	1901–1911.	1891–1901.	1881–1891.	1881–1931.
1	2	3	4	5	6	7	8	9	10	11	12	13	14
Total ..	*163,327*	*10,000*	*10,000*	*10,000*	*10,000*	*10,000*	*10,000*	— *0·3*	— *6·4*	— *3·1*	+ *4·4*	— *2·9*	— *9·1*
Hindu	146,007	8,940	7,733	7,939	8,849	} 9,063	9,113	— 1·0 {	— 8·8	— 13·1 }	+ 4·0	— 3·5	—10·1
Animistic	..	..	1,265	1,099	183 }				+ 7·8	+ 481·8 }			
Muslim	13,777	843	795	751	756	732	703	+ 5·8	— 0·9	— 3·7	+ 7·8	+ 1·0	+ 9·9
Christian	3,425	210	194	203	204	196	177	+ 7·6	— 10·4	— 3·5	+ 8·6	+ 7·6	+ 8·7
† Jain	83	5	12	6	6	7	6	— 59	+ 108·2	— 9·3	— 6·1	+ 15·2	— 16
† Buddist	3	..	1	..	..	..	..	— 79	..	..	..	..	
† Parsi	27	2	..	2	2	2	1	*	*	— 17·1	+ 5·1	+ 85·7	+ 29
† Agnostic	5	..	..	..	..	..	..	*	..	..	..	..	*

* The strict mathematical figure is infinity. With such small totals, percentages are really worthless.
† The figures relating to these castes are based upon the small population returns. They are only of academic interest but of no real value.

ii.—Christians—Number and Variation.

Year.	Actual population.	Variation. Period.	Percentage.
1	2	3	4
1881	3,152	1881–1891	+ 7·6
1891	3,392	1891–1901	+ 8·6
1901	3,683	1901–1911	— 3·5
1911	3,553	1911–1921	— 10·4
1921	3,182	1921–1931	+ 7·6
1931	3,425	1881–1931	+ 8·7

iii.—Religions of Urban and Rural Population.

Province.	Number per 10,000 of urban population who are Hindu.	Muslim.	Christian.	Jain.	Parsi.	Number per 10,000 of rural population who are Hindu.	Muslim.	Christian.	Animistic.	Jain.	Buddhis
1	2	3	4	5	6	7	8	9	10	11	12
Coorg ..	6,553	2,502	866	51	28	9,092	738	168	..	2	..

CHAPTER XII.

CASTE, TRIBE, RACE OR NATIONALITY.

Reference to statistics. THIS final chapter of the report is devoted exclusively to the examination of returns relating to the caste, tribe, race or nationality of the people enumerated. The figures are compiled in Imperial Tables XVII and XVIII. Similar figures for Europeans and Anglo-Indians are dealt with in Imperial Table XIX.

Value of statistics. 2. In dealing with the value of the statistics in 1921 in respect of this chapter, it has been clearly pointed out that the figures pertaining to Kodagas, Amma Kodagas, Jama Kodagas and Brahmans, etc., are vitiated by several inaccuracies. Consequently, it serves no useful purpose to compare the figures of this census with that of 1921 census. The total population of 'Kodagas' as disclosed in the census returns of 1931, is 41,026. Though special instructions were issued to exclude from this category all persons who are virtually not Coorgs by caste, it is believed that Jama Coorgs (who are not Coorgs by race) of Somwarpet and Sunticoppa Nads, who produced 'Nirupas' in which they were described as 'Kodagas', were entered as such in the census schedules. The number of such persons may not exceed a thousand at the outside. Subject to this discrepancy, the figures for this community may be considered as accurate. Amma Coorgs number 666, Brahmans of all kinds number 2,723. The Gaudas, another important community, who number 14,016, show an increase of 753. Holeyas come next; they numbered 18,350 in 1921, 147 Madigas, however, having been excluded and shown separately. But during the last census, the number of Holeyas is only 320. Presumably, Adi-Dravidas, Adiyas, Balagai and Panchama, who are now separately shown were included among Holeyas in 1921. When all the above four castes are treated as Holeyas, the total works out to 20,078.

Yeravas. 3. The Yeravas form another important community in Coorg. They number 12,810 and show a decrease of 1,198 when compared with the figure of last census. The southernmost portions of Coorg and portions of Mysore and Wynad adjoining the Coorg boundary in the south, are the usual place of residence of this constantly moving tribe. February, the month in which the final census took place, being the time when agricultural work was almost over, the Yeravas who mostly belong to the working class, were moving about among their kinsmen in Mysore and Wynad. The decrease may, therefore, be due to such movements. There are no signs of this tribe dwindling.

Other minor castes. 4. Among other minor communities, Mappillas record a further increase of 16 per cent. The next notable increase is among Pales, who have risen from 2,299 to 3,192. They are mostly a working class from outside the Province and they must have come in larger numbers in 1931. Vakkaligas, Indian Christians and Malayas also show slight increase over the figures for 1921. A decrease by nearly half is seen in the Lingayat community. This may probably be due to inaccurate enumeration in 1921. A similar decrease is noticed among Maratha, where the fall is nearly 70 per cent. The other minor decreases are among Kurubas and Medas.

Europeans and Anglo-Indians. 5. Imperial Table XIX, deals with Europeans and Anglo-Indians by age, race and sect. Only 16 Europeans out of 138 are described as non-British subjects. The number of Europeans and British subjects show a decrease from 250 to 138, while Anglo-Indians record an increase from 47 to 84.

IMPERIAL TABLES

TABLE I

Area, Houses and Population.

Province.	Area in square miles.	Towns.	Villages.	Occupied Houses. Total.	In towns.	In villages.	Population. Persons. Total.	Urban.	Rural.	Males. Total.	Urban.	Rural.	Females. Total.	Urban.	Rural.
1	2	3	4	5	6	7	8	9	10	11	12	13	14	15	16
Coorg	* 1,582	2	378	33,906	1,942	31,964	**163,327**	9,827	153,500	**90,575**	5,848	84,727	**72,752**	3,979	68,773

* The revised area of the Province according to computation from the latest surveys is 1593 sq. miles.

TABLE II

Variation in Population since 1891.

Province.	Persons. 1931.	1921.	1911.	1901.	1891.	Variation. 1921 to 1931.	1911 to 1921.	1901 to 1911.	1891 to 1901.	Net variation in period 1891 to 1931	Males. 1931.	1921.	1911.	1901.	1891.	Females. 1931.	1921.	1911.	1901.	1891.
1	2	3	4	5	6	7	8	9	10	11	12	13	14	15	16	17	18	19	20	21
Coorg ..	**163,327**	163,838	174,976	180,607	173,055	— 511	— 11,138	— 5,631	+ 7,552	— 9,728	**90,575**	89,501	97,279	100,258	95,907	**72,752**	74,337	77,697	80,349	77,148

TABLE III

Towns and Villages classified by Population.

Province.	Total number of inhabited towns and villages.	Population.	Under 500. Number.	Population.	500—1,000. Number.	Population.	1,000—2,000. Number.	Population.	2,000—5,000. Number.	Population.	5,000—10,000. Number.	Population.	10,000—20,000. Number.	Population.	20,000—50,000. Number.	Population.	50,000—100,000. Number.	Population.	100,000 and over. Number.	Population.	Encampments, Boat and Railway population unclassed.
1	2	3	4	5	6	7	8	9	10	11	12	13	14	15	16	17	18	19	20	21	22
Coorg	380	163,327	289	66,948	89	59,541	20	26,218	1	3,832	1	5,995	..	..	..	..	..	..	..	..	795

TABLE IV

Towns classified by Population with variation for fifty years.

Town.	Description of Town.	Population. 1931.	1921.	1911.	1901.	1891.	1881.	Variation. 1921 to 1931.	1911 to 1921.	1901 to 1911.	1891 to 1901.	1881 to 1891.	Variation in period 1881 to 1931.	Males. 1931.	1921.	1911.	Females. 1931.	1921.	1911.
1	2	3	4	5	6	7	8	9	10	11	12	13	14	15	16	17	18	19	20
1. Mercara	Municipality.	**5,995**	5,675	6,269	6,732	7,034	8,383	+ 320	— 594	— 463	— 302	— 1,349	— 2,388	**3,427**	3,313	3,692	**2,568**	2,362	2,577
2. Virarajendrapet ..	Do.	**3,832**	3,166	3,712	4,283	4,447	4,576	+ 666	— 546	— 571	— 164	— 129	— 744	**2,421**	1,967	2,205	**1,411**	1,199	1,507

TABLE V

Towns arranged territorially with Population by Religion.

Province and Town.	Town, Municipality, etc.	Population. Persons.	Population. Males.	Population. Females.	Hindu. Persons.	Hindu. Males.	Hindu. Females.	Muslim. Persons.	Muslim. Males.	Muslim. Females.	Christian. Persons.	Christian. Males.	Christian. Females.
1	2	3	4	5	6	7	8	9	10	11	12	13	14
Total		***9,827***	***5,848***	***3,979***	***6,440***	***3,805***	***2,635***	***2,459***	***1,545***	***914***	***851***	***464***	***387***
Coorg—													
Mercara	M.	**5,995**	3,427	2,568	**4,277**	2,460	1,817	**1,175**	677	498	**527**	283	244
Virarajendrapet ..	M.	**3,832**	2,421	1,411	**2,163**	1,345	818	**1,284**	868	416	**324**	181	143

Province and Town.	Jain. Persons.	Jain. Males.	Jain. Females.	Buddhist. Persons.	Buddhist. Males.	Buddhist. Females.	Jew. Persons.	Jew. Males.	Jew. Females.	Zoroastrian (Parsi). Persons.	Zoroastrian (Parsi). Males.	Zoroastrian (Parsi). Females.	Others. Persons.	Others. Males.	Others. Females.
	15	16	17	18	19	20	21	22	23	24	25	26	27	28	29
Total	***50***	***22***	***28***	..	..	..	..	..	..	***27***	***12***	***15***	..	..	..
Coorg—															
Mercara	**1**	1	..	..	..	..	..	..	..	**15**	6	9	..	..	..
Virarajendrapet ..	**49**	21	28	..	..	..	..	..	..	**12**	6	6	..	..	..

TABLE VI

Birthplace.

Province, State or Country where born.	Persons.	Males.	Females.
1	2	3	4
Total ..	***163,327***	***90,575***	***72,752***
A I.—Born within the Province (Coorg)	***124,609***	***64,926***	***59,683***
A II.—Born in Provinces and States beyond the Province	***38,619***	***25,596***	***13,023***
(*a*) Adjacent Provinces and States	**38,304**	25,362	12,942
i. British Territory (Madras)	**25,333**	18,142	7,191
ii. State (Mysore)	**12,971**	7,220	5,751
(*b*) Other Provinces and States	**299**	225	74
i. British Territory	**179**	143	36
Burma	**7**	6	1
Elsewhere in British India	**172**	137	35
ii. States	**120**	82	38
Travancore	**24**	18	6
Cochin	**71**	50	21
Pudukkottai	**1**	..	1
Hyderabad	**21**	11	10
Other Indian States	**3**	3	..
(*c*) India unspecified	**7**	1	6
(*d*) French and Portuguese Settlements	**9**	8	1
B.—Born in other Asiatic Countries	***13***	9	***4***
(*a*) Within British Dominions (Ceylon)	**9**	6	3
(*b*) Outside British Dominions	**3**	3	..
i. China	**1**	1	..
ii. Afghanistan	**2**	2	..
(*c*) Asia unspecified	**1**	..	1
C.—Born in Europe	***72***	***39***	***33***
(*a*) United Kingdom and Ireland	**66**	37	29
(*b*) Continental Europe (France)	**6**	2	4
D.—Born in Africa (unspecified)	***7***	***3***	***4***
E.—Born in America	***5***	***2***	***3***
(*a*) Within British Dominions (Canada)	**4**	1	3
(*b*) Outside British Dominions (U.S.A.)	**1**	1	..
F.—Born in Australasia (unspecified)	***2***	..	***2***

TABLE VII

Age, Sex and Civil Condition.

Religion.	Age.	Population. Persons.	Population. Males.	Population. Females.	Unmarried. Persons.	Unmarried. Males.	Unmarried. Females.	Married. Persons.	Married. Males.	Married. Females.	Widowed. Persons.	Widowed. Males.	Widowed. Females.
1		2	3	4	5	6	7	8	9	10	11	12	13
ALL RELIGIONS.	TOTAL ..	*163,327*	*90,575*	*72,752*	*82,535*	*50,212*	*32,323*	*64,417*	*35,582*	*28,835*	*16,375*	*4,781*	*11,594*
	0–1 ..	**4,313**	2,127	2,186	**4,308**	2,126	2,182	**5**	1	4	..	..	..
	1–2 ..	**4,378**	2,184	2,194	**4,373**	2,183	2,190	**5**	1	4	..	..	..
	2–3 ..	**3,931**	1,911	2,020	**3,923**	1,908	2,015	**8**	3	5	..	..	..
	3–4 ..	**3,498**	1,721	1,777	**3,493**	1,719	1,774	**5**	2	3	..	..	..
	4–5 ..	**3,402**	1,725	1,677	**3,391**	1,721	1,670	**9**	4	5	**2**	..	2
	TOTAL 0–5.	*19,522*	*9,668*	*9,854*	*19,488*	*9,657*	*9,831*	*32*	*11*	*21*	*2*	..	*2*
	5–10 ..	**18,616**	9,527	9,089	**18,486**	9,491	8,995	**122**	36	86	**8**	..	8
	10–15 ..	**18,954**	9,993	8,961	**18,367**	9,925	8,442	**559**	66	493	**28**	2	26
	15–20 ..	**16,639**	9,129	7,510	**11,473**	8,232	3,241	**4,923**	859	4,064	**243**	38	205
	20–25 ..	**17,991**	9,879	8,112	**8,525**	7,133	1,392	**8,888**	2,612	6,276	**578**	134	444
	25–30 ..	**16,867**	9,740	7,127	**3,352**	3,185	167	**12,166**	6,111	6,055	**1,349**	444	905
	30–35 ..	**15,216**	9,175	6,041	**1,650**	1,557	93	**11,804**	7,001	4,803	**1,762**	617	1,145
	35–40 ..	**11,435**	7,164	4,271	**540**	489	51	**8,777**	5,991	2,786	**2,118**	684	1,434
	40–45 ..	**9,021**	5,607	3,414	**304**	259	45	**6,654**	4,733	1,921	**2,063**	615	1,448
	45–50 ..	**6,281**	3,771	2,510	**142**	117	25	**4,161**	3,119	1,042	**1,978**	535	1,443
	50–55 ..	**4,801**	2,784	2,017	**92**	77	15	**2,912**	2,239	673	**1,797**	468	1,329
	55–60 ..	**3,063**	1,634	1,429	**45**	36	9	**1,521**	1,215	306	**1,497**	383	1,114
	60–65 ..	**2,346**	1,213	1,133	**30**	22	8	**1,043**	857	186	**1,273**	334	939
	65–70 ..	**1,130**	585	545	**19**	16	3	**421**	360	61	**690**	209	481
	70 and over.	**1,445**	706	739	**22**	16	6	**434**	372	62	**989**	318	671
HINDU.	TOTAL ..	*146,007*	*79,559*	*66,448*	*74,180*	*44,310*	*29,870*	*56,846*	*30,830*	*26,016*	*14,981*	*4,419*	*10,562*
	0–1 ..	**3,953**	1,943	2,010	**3,948**	1,942	2,006	**5**	1	4	..	..	..
	1–2 ..	**4,010**	1,993	2,017	**4,005**	1,992	2,013	**5**	1	4	..	..	..
	2–3 ..	**3,600**	1,742	1,858	**3,594**	1,739	1,855	**6**	3	3	..	..	..
	3–4 ..	**3,212**	1,571	1,641	**3,207**	1,569	1,638	**5**	2	3	..	..	..
	4–5 ..	**3,139**	1,586	1,553	**3,128**	1,582	1,546	**9**	4	5	**2**	..	2
	TOTAL 0–5.	*17,914*	*8,835*	*9,079*	*17,882*	*8,824*	*9,058*	*30*	*11*	*19*	*2*	..	*2*
	5–10 ..	**17,040**	8,672	8,368	**16,926**	8,638	8,288	**106**	34	72	**8**	..	8
	10–15 ..	**17,159**	8,949	8,210	**16,666**	8,886	7,780	**471**	61	410	**22**	2	20
	15–20 ..	**14,655**	7,845	6,810	**10,110**	7,062	3,048	**4,335**	750	3,585	**210**	33	177
	20–25 ..	**15,773**	8,417	7,356	**7,363**	6,038	1,325	**7,899**	2,262	5,637	**511**	117	394
	25–30 ..	**14,843**	8,356	6,487	**2,808**	2,661	147	**10,806**	5,291	5,515	**1,229**	404	825
	30–35 ..	**13,410**	7,916	5,494	**1,387**	1,305	82	**10,412**	6,043	4,369	**1,611**	568	1,043
	35–40 ..	**10,132**	6,240	3,892	**466**	420	46	**7,727**	5,189	2,538	**1,939**	631	1,308
	40–45 ..	**8,052**	4,928*	3,124	**273**	232	41	**5,883**	4,127*	1,756	**1,896**	569	1,327
	45–50 ..	**5,594**	3,317	2,277	**122**	102	20	**3,662**	2,715	947	**1,810**	500	1,310
	50–55 ..	**4,276**	2,444	1,832	**78**	66	12	**2,548**	1,943	605	**1,650**	435	1,215
	55–60 ..	**2,739**	1,427	1,312	**39**	31	8	**1,319**	1,039	280	**1,381**	357	1,024
	60–65 ..	**2,111**	1,074	1,037	**26**	20	6	**911**	739	172	**1,174**	315	859
	65–70 ..	**1,018**	522	496	**16**	13	3	**369**	314	55	**633**	195	438
	70 and over.	**1,291**	617	674	**18**	12	6	**368**	312	56	**905**	293	612
MUSLIM.	TOTAL ..	*13,777*	*8,943*	*4,834*	*6,554*	*4,725*	*1,829*	*6,153*	*3,952*	*2,201*	*1,070*	*266*	*804*
	0–1 ..	**274**	137	137	**274**	137	137	..	..	..	..	..	..
	1–2 ..	**280**	140	140	**280**	140	140	..	..	..	..	..	..
	2–3 ..	**250**	124	126	**248**	124	124	**2**	..	2	..	..	..
	3–4 ..	**219**	114	105	**219**	114	105	..	..	..	..	..	..
	4–5 ..	**199**	106	93	**199**	106	93	..	..	..	..	..	..
	TOTAL 0–5.	*1,222*	*621*	*601*	*1,220*	*621*	*599*	*2*	..	*2*	..	..	..
	5–10 ..	**1,226**	671	555	**1,211**	669	542	**15**	2	13	..	..	..
	10–15 ..	**1,424**	842	582	**1,339**	838	501	**79**	4	75	**6**	..	6
	15–20 ..	**1,621**	1,074	547	**1,104**	976	128	**488**	94	394	**29**	4	25
	20–25 ..	**1,821**	1,226	595	**946**	910	36	**819**	302	517	**56**	14	42
	25–30 ..	**1,635**	1,151	484	**434**	424	10	**1,106**	693	413	**95**	34	61
	30–35 ..	**1,450**	1,040	410	**204**	197	7	**1,133**	805	328	**113**	38	75
	35–40 ..	**1,044**	757	287	**52**	49	3	**858**	667	191	**134**	41	93
	40–45 ..	**767**	552	215	**18**	17	1	**621**	501	120	**128**	34	94
	45–50 ..	**541**	367	174	**8**	7	1	**403**	337	66	**130**	23	107
	50–55 ..	**414**	273	141	**7**	7	..	**293**	244	49	**114**	22	92
	55–60 ..	**240**	153	87	**2**	2	..	**152**	134	18	**86**	17	69
	60–65 ..	**174**	99	75	**3**	2	1	**96**	86	10	**75**	11	64
	65–70 ..	**81**	45	36	**2**	2	..	**38**	35	3	**41**	8	33
	70 and over.	**117**	72	45	**4**	4	..	**50**	48	2	**63**	20	43

* Includes one Brahmo.

TABLE VII

Age, Sex and Civil Condition—*cont.*

Religion.	Age.	Population.			Unmarried.			Married.			Widowed.		
		Persons.	Males.	Females.	Persons.	Males.	Females.	Persons.	Males.	Females.	Persons.	Males.	Females.
	1	2	3	4	5	6	7	8	9	10	11	12	13
Christian.	Total ..	***3,430*** †	***2,015***	***1,415***	***1,741***	***1,142***	***599***	***1,377***	***780***	***597***	***312***	***93***	***219***
	0–1 ..	**81**	45	36	**81**	45	36	..	..	..	..	..	..
	1–2 ..	**84**	48	36	**84**	48	36	..	..	..	..	..	..
	2–3 ..	**78**	43	35	**78**	43	35	..	..	..	..	..	..
	3–4 ..	**66**	35	31	**66**	35	31	..	..	..	..	..	..
	4–5 ..	**60**	32	28	**60**	32	28	..	..	..	..	..	..
	Total 0–5.	***369***	***203***	***166***	***369***	***203***	***166***	..	..	..	..	..	..
	5–10 ..	**337**	179	158	**337**	179	158	..	..	..	..	..	..
	10–15 ..	**357**	196	161	**350**	195	155	**7**	1	6	..	..	..
	15–20 ..	**351**	205	146	**254**	190	64	**93**	14	79	**4**	1	3
	20–25 ..	**388**	232	156	**213**	183	30	**165**	46	119	**10**	3	7
	25–30 ..	**376**	226	150	**105**	97	8	**247**	123	124	**24**	6	18
	30–35 ..	**348**	214	134	**57**	53	4	**254**	150	104	**37**	11	26
	35–40 ..	**251**	162	89	**19**	17	2	**189**	133	56	**43**	12	31
	40–45 ..	**196**	123	73	**12**	9	3	**146**	103	43	**38**	11	27
	45–50 ..	**142**	85	57	**12**	8	4	**93**	65	28	**37**	12	25
	50–55 ..	**108**	64	44	**7**	4	3	**70**	51	19	**31**	9	22
	55–60 ..	**82**	53	29	**4**	3	1	**49**	41	8	**29**	9	20
	60–65 ..	**60**	39	21	**1**	..	1	**35**	31	4	**24**	8	16
	65–70 ..	**29**	17	12	**1**	1	..	**13**	10	3	**15**	6	9
	70 and over.	**38**	17	19	..	..	..	**16**	12	4	**20**	5	15
Jain.	Total ..	***83***	***43***	***40***	***41***	***26***	***15***	***33***	***15***	***18***	***9***	***2***	***7***
	0–1 ..	**5**	2	3	**5**	2	3	..	..	..	..	..	..
	1–2 ..	**4**	3	1	**4**	3	1	..	..	..	..	..	..
	2–3 ..	**3**	2	1	**3**	2	1	..	..	..	..	..	..
	3–4 ..	**1**	1	..	**1**	1	..	..	..	..	..	..	..
	4–5 ..	**1**	..	1	**1**	..	1	..	..	..	..	..	..
	Total 0–5.	***14***	***8***	***6***	***14***	***8***	***6***	..	..	..	..	..	..
	5–10 ..	**9**	3	6	**8**	3	5	**1**	..	1	..	..	..
	10–15 ..	**11**	5	6	**9**	5	4	**2**	..	2	..	..	..
	15–20 ..	**10**	4	6	**3**	3	..	**7**	1	6	..	..	..
	20–25 ..	**8**	4	4	**2**	2	..	**5**	2	3	**1**	..	1
	25–30 ..	**9**	6	3	**2**	2	..	**6**	4	2	**1**	..	1
	30–35 ..	**4**	1	3	..	..	..	**3**	1	2	**1**	..	1
	35–40 ..	**6**	3	3	**2**	2	..	**2**	1	1	**2**	..	2
	40–45 ..	**4**	4	..	**1**	1	..	**2**	2	..	**1**	1	..
	45–50 ..	**2**	..	2	..	..	..	**1**	..	1	**1**	..	1
	50–55 ..	**2**	2	..	..	..	..	**1**	1	..	**1**	1	..
	55–60 ..	**2**	1	1	..	..	..	**1**	1	..	**1**	..	1
	60–65 ..	**1**	1	..	..	..	..	**1**	1	..	..	..	..
	65–70 ..	**1**	1	..	..	..	..	**1**	1	..	..	..	..
	70 and over.	..	..	..	..	..	..	..	..	..	..	..	..
Zoroastrian (Parsi).	Total ..	***27***	***12***	***15***	***17***	***7***	***10***	***7***	***4***	***3***	***3***	***1***	***2***
	0–1 ..	..	..	..	..	..	..	..	..	..	..	..	..
	1–2 ..	..	..	..	..	..	..	..	..	..	..	..	..
	2–3 ..	..	..	..	..	..	..	..	..	..	..	..	..
	3–4 ..	..	..	..	..	..	..	..	..	..	..	..	..
	4–5 ..	**3**	1	2	**3**	1	2	..	..	..	..	..	..
	Total 0–5.	***3***	***1***	***2***	***3***	***1***	***2***	..	..	..	..	..	..
	5–10 ..	**4**	2	2	**4**	2	2	..	..	..	..	..	..
	10–15 ..	**3**	1	2	**3**	1	2	..	..	..	..	..	..
	15–20 ..	**2**	1	1	**2**	1	1	..	..	..	..	..	..
	20–25 ..	**1**	..	1	**1**	..	1	..	..	..	..	..	..
	25–30 ..	**3**	..	3	**2**	..	2	**1**	..	1	..	..	..
	30–35 ..	**2**	2	..	**1**	1	..	**1**	1	..	..	..	..
	35–40 ..	**2**	2	..	**1**	1	..	**1**	1	..	..	..	..
	40–45 ..	**2**	..	2	..	..	..	**2**	..	2	..	..	..
	45–50 ..	**2**	2	..	..	..	..	**2**	2	..	..	..	..
	50–55 ..	**1**	1	..	..	..	..	..	..	..	**1**	1	..
	55–60 ..	..	..	..	..	..	..	..	..	..	..	..	..
	60–65 ..	..	..	..	..	..	..	..	..	..	..	..	..
	65–70 ..	**1**	..	1	..	..	..	..	..	..	**1**	..	1
	70 and over.	**1**	..	1	..	..	..	..	..	..	**1**	..	1

† 5 persons (3 males and 2 females) returned under 'Indefinite Beliefs' in Table XVI have been classed as Christians for the purpose of this table.

TABLE VII

Age, Sex and Civil Condition—*cont.*

Religion.	Age.	Population.			Unmarried.			Married.			Widowed.		
		Persons.	Males.	Females.	Persons.	Males.	Females.	Persons.	Males.	Females.	Persons.	Males.	Females.
	1	2	3	4	5	6	7	8	9	10	11	12	13
Buddhist.	Total ..	*3*	*3*	..	*2*	*2*	..	*1*	*1*	..	..	..	..
	0–1 ..	..	..	..	..	..	..	..	..	..	..	..	..
	1–2 ..	..	..	..	..	..	..	..	..	..	..	..	..
	2–3 ..	..	..	..	..	..	..	..	..	..	..	..	..
	3–4 ..	..	..	..	..	..	..	..	..	..	..	..	..
	4–5 ..	..	..	..	..	..	..	..	..	..	..	..	..
	Total 0–5.	..	..	..	..	..	..	..	..	..	..	..	..
	5–10 ..	..	..	..	..	..	..	..	..	..	..	..	..
	10–15 ..	..	..	..	..	..	..	..	..	..	..	..	..
	15–20 ..	..	..	..	..	..	..	..	..	..	..	..	..
	20–25 ..	..	..	..	..	..	..	..	..	..	..	..	..
	25–30 ..	1	1	..	1	1	..	..	..	..	..	..	..
	30–35 ..	2	2	..	1	1	..	1	1	..	..	..	..
	35–40 ..	..	..	..	..	..	..	..	..	..	..	..	..
	40–45 ..	..	..	..	..	..	..	..	..	..	..	..	..
	45–50 ..	..	..	..	..	..	..	..	..	..	..	..	..
	50–55 ..	..	..	..	..	..	..	..	..	..	..	..	..
	55–60 ..	..	..	..	..	..	..	..	..	..	..	..	..
	60–65 ..	..	..	..	..	..	..	..	..	..	..	..	..
	65–70 ..	..	..	..	..	..	..	..	..	..	..	..	..
	70 and over.	..	..	..	..	..	..	..	..	..	..	..	..

TABLE VIII

Civil condition by age for selected Communities.

Race, Tribe or Caste.	Sex.	Population.	Unmarried. Total.	0 to 6.	7 to 13.	14 to 16.	17 to 23.	24 to 43.	44 and over.	Married. Total.	0 to 6.	7 to 13.	14 to 16.	17 to 23.	24 to 43.	44 and over.	Widowed. Total.	0 to 6.	7 to 13.	14 to 16.	17 to 23.	24 to 43.	44 and over.
1	2	3	4	5	6	7	8	9	10	11	12	13	14	15	16	17	18	19	20	21	22	23	24
Arya Valsya (Komati)	Males ..	100	49	15	17	5	8	4	..	46	..	1	1	6	29	9	5	..	..	..	..	1	4
	Females.	111	43	26	16	1	..	..	..	51	..	4	9	19	17	2	17	..	..	..	1	4	12
Maratha	Males ..	360	169	8	24	24	50	61	2	172	..	1	1	10	127	33	19	..	..	..	..	7	12
	Females.	180	41	12	17	8	1	3	..	99	..	4	4	23	59	9	40	..	1	..	6	11	22
Nayar	Males ..	1,100	539	24	39	35	191	238	12	505	..	1	1	16	368	119	56	..	..	..	..	36	20
	Females.	178	74	32	26	11	4	1	..	86	..	2	3	19	54	8	18	..	..	1	1	7	9
Labbai	Males ..	126	62	15	13	9	12	13	..	60	..	..	..	3	41	16	4	..	..	..	..	2	2
	Females.	92	31	14	13	3	1	..	..	39	..	1	3	12	20	3	22	..	..	..	3	9	10
Bant	Males ..	872	504	69	94	53	116	165	7	335	..	..	..	10	237	88	33	..	..	..	..	19	14
	Females.	497	213	90	75	24	21	1	2	205	1	4	4	49	131	16	79	..	..	..	1	35	43
Brahman-Kanarese.	Males ..	685	376	83	112	48	89	41	3	254	..	1	..	18	167	68	55	..	..	..	1	18	36
	Females.	573	209	90	105	12	1	1	..	213	..	5	28	70	93	17	151	..	..	..	5	65	81
Golla	Males ..	289	158	44	48	17	28	20	1	104	..	..	..	6	69	29	27	..	..	..	..	13	14
	Females.	231	94	39	44	8	2	1	..	90	..	2	4	24	53	7	47	..	..	..	1	14	32
Holeya	Males ..	185	90	24	26	10	22	7	1	86	..	..	..	5	65	16	9	..	..	..	..	5	4
	Females.	135	63	22	25	3	7	5	1	59	..	1	..	22	28	8	13	..	..	..	1	7	5
Mappilla	Males ..	6,051	3,280	464	642	477	942	725	10	2,664	..	..	3	131	1,949	581	127	..	..	..	5	80	42
	Females.	2,753	1,060	433	469	107	34	16	1	1,316	1	19	81	396	725	94	377	..	..	6	24	153	194
Kudiya	Males ..	270	156	52	49	17	26	11	1	97	..	..	..	7	64	26	17	..	..	..	..	9	8
	Females.	279	123	61	43	8	10	1	..	106	..	2	1	26	66	11	50	..	..	..	1	18	31
Kuruba	Males ..	3,710	1,900	638	528	199	307	220	8	1,571	1	1	3	75	1,014	477	239	..	..	..	1	130	108
	Females.	3,157	1,335	594	481	140	92	26	2	1,536	..	12	30	843	1,008	148	286	1	1	1	11	104	168
Palo	Males ..	2,128	991	133	225	136	282	210	5	1,026	..	2	2	59	797	166	111	..	..	..	1	78	32
	Females.	1,064	384	157	162	38	19	8	..	531	..	4	23	163	322	19	149	..	1	..	12	72	64
Vakkaliga	Males ..	4,233	2,394	519	668	351	508	333	15	1,596	3	1	1	96	1,123	372	243	..	..	..	6	114	123
	Females.	3,715	1,541	551	678	216	80	15	1	1,276	..	10	50	395	744	77	398	..	1	4	32	420	441
Yerava	Males ..	6,763	3,216	1,223	922	347	477	235	12	3,119	1	10	3	131	2,085	889	428	..	..	..	7	240	181
	Females.	6,047	2,498	1,218	841	252	145	39	3	3,012	3	13	40	637	2,001	319	536	..	1	..	28	150	357
Lingayat	Males ..	2,250	1,357	279	424	173	237	230	14	708	3	2	..	29	471	203	185	..	..	..	1	83	101
	Females.	2,818	1,134	385	562	138	35	12	2	912	1	6	70	303	482	50	772	..	..	3	38	361	370
Gauda	Males ..	7,388	4,233	1,175	1,223	452	846	510	27	2,773	..	7	8	116	1815	827	382	..	..	1	8	152	221
	Females.	6,628	3,184	1,260	1,209	418	258	27	12	2,550	2	7	41	644	1,600	256	394	..	1	..	11	304	578
Panchama	Males ..	10,971	5,641	1,245	1,614	772	1,113	864	33	4,684	..	7	18	244	3,497	918	646	..	..	1	10	360	275
	Females.	8,600	3,511	1,313	1,545	303	211	76	3	3,679	2	6	153	1,015	2,278	225	1,410	..	..	11	69	724	606
Kodaga	Males ..	20,752	13,097	3,680	4,124	1,452	2,380	1,394	67	6,708	1	9	7	203	4,102	2,386	947	..	..	..	6	339	602
	Females.	20,274	10,524	3,585	4,036	1,408	1,356	119	20	6,888	6	6	39	1,385	4,407	1,045	2,862	1	2	3	30	953	1,873
Amma Kodaga ..	Males ..	336	202	55	52	30	40	24	1	114	..	..	..	6	68	40	20	..	..	..	..	0	11
	Females.	330	166	64	61	16	25	..	..	115	..	..	..	25	78	12	49	..	..	..	2	11	36
Boya	Males ..	236	123	30	32	14	28	19	..	86	..	..	1	3	70	12	17	..	..	..	..	10	7
	Females.	217	86	38	27	9	9	2	1	81	..	..	1	27	49	4	50	..	..	..	3	27	20
Madiga	Males ..	122	62	25	16	10	5	6	..	56	..	..	..	5	40	11	4	..	..	..	..	3	1
	Females.	95	45	13	26	1	5	..	..	35	..	..	3	9	21	2	15	..	..	..	..	8	7
Paraiyan	Males ..	194	38	22	24	10	22	10	..	85	..	..	..	5	68	12	11	..	..	..	1	7	3
	Females.	156	56	28	20	4	3	1	..	84	..	..	2	16	62	4	16	..	..	..	2	8	6
Telaga	Males ..	142	84	20	30	7	18	8	1	47	..	..	1	2	30	14	11	..	..	..	..	2	9
	Females.	138	56	26	18	6	4	..	..	48	..	..	2	12	31	3	34	..	..	..	..	15	19

The communities in this table are arranged in the order of frequency of child marriage, i.e., according to the proportion which the number in each community of married females under 13 years of age bears to its total female population.

TABLE IX

Infirmities—Part I—Distribution by Age.

Age.	Population Afflicted.			Insane.			Deafmutes.			Blind.			Lepers.		
	Persons.	Males.	Females.	Persons.	Males.	Females.	Persons.	Males.	Females.	Persons.	Males.	Females.	Persons.	Males.	Females.
1	2	3	4	5	6	7	8	9	10	11	12	13	14	15	16
Total ..	*248*	*136*	*112*	*31*	*13*	*18*	*101*	*55*	*46*	*100*	*58*	*42*	*17*	*11*	*6*
0—1	..	..	..	..	..	..	..	..	..	..	..	..	..	..	..
1—2	..	..	..	..	..	..	..	..	..	..	..	..	..	..	..
2—3	..	..	..	..	..	..	..	..	..	..	..	..	..	..	..
3—4	1	..	1	..	..	..	..	..	..	1	..	1	..	..	..
4—5	4	1	3	1	1	..	2	..	2	1	..	1	..	..	..
Total 0—5 ..	*5*	*1*	*4*	*1*	*1*	..	*2*	..	*2*	*2*	..	*2*	..	..	..
5—10	18	9	9	2	1	1	13	7	6	4	2	2	..	..	..
10—15	29	18	11	3	2	1	15	8	7	9	7	2	2	1	1
15—20	31	20	11	3	1	2	16	11	5	11	8	3	1	..	1
20—25	28	19	9	2	1	1	15	11	4	9	6	3	2	1	1
25—30	22	9	13	3	..	3	12	6	6	6	2	4	1	1	..
30—35	24	9	15	5	1	4	11	5	6	6	2	4	2	1	1
35—40	15	8	7	4	1	3	4	2	2	5	3	2	2	2	..
40—45	11	6	5	2	2	..	5	2	3	4	2	2	..	..	..
45—50	16	8	8	2	1	1	4	1	3	8	5	3	2	1	1
50—55	16	9	7	2	1	1	3	1	2	9	6	3	2	1	1
55—60	11	8	3	1	1	..	1	1	..	8	5	3	1	1	..
60—65	9	5	4	1	..	1	..	..	..	7	4	3	1	1	..
65—70	6	3	3	..	..	..	..	..	..	6	3	3	..	..	..
70 and over	7	4	3	..	..	..	..	..	..	6	3	3	1	1	..

Note.—One male was returned as suffering from double infirmity, insanity and deafmutism. This explains the difference between the total persons afflicted in columns 2 and 3 and the total of the figures under each infirmity.

For figures of Table IX—Part II—Distribution by District, please see figures against 'Total' at the beginning of the above statement.

TABLE X *

Occupation or Means of Livelihood.

	Persons.	Males.	Females.
Total population	163,327	90,575	72,752
,, earners	84,573	62,345	22,228
,, working dependents ..	27,100	1,778	25,322
,, non-working dependents	51,654	26,452	25,202

Group number.	Occupation.	Province. Total following occupation.	As principal occupation. Males.	As principal occupation. Females.	As working dependents. Males.	As working dependents. Females.	As subsidiary to other occupation. Males.	As subsidiary to other occupation. Females.
1	2	3	4	5	6	7	8	9
	Grand total	*125,228*	*62,345*	*22,228*	*1,778*	*25,322*	*5,433*	*8,122*
	Class A.—Production of Raw Materials ..	*62,631*	*44,394*	*15,756*	*512*	*154*	*1,568*	*247*
	SUB-CLASS I.—EXPLOITATION OF ANIMALS AND VEGETATION ..	*62,631*	*44,394*	*15,756*	*512*	*154*	*1,568*	*247*
	Order 1.—*Pasture and Agriculture* ..	*62,580*	*44,367*	*15,751*	*512*	*137*	*1,566*	*247*
	(*a*) Cultivation	*48,461*	*35,437*	*11,207*	*224*	*114*	*1,271*	*208*
1	Non-cultivating proprietors taking rent in money or kind	2,186	1,170	603	9	2	398	4
5	Cultivating owners	25,609	21,648	3,707	23	7	222	2
6	Tenant cultivators	1,257	1,119	42	71	5	18	2
6a	Non-cultivating tenants	601	372	212	..	2	14	1
7	Agricultural labourers	18,808	11,128	6,643	121	98	619	199
	(*b*) Cultivation of special crops, fruit, etc. (Planters, managers, clerks and labourers)	*13,156*	*8,341*	*4,531*	*26*	*17*	*203*	*38*
11	Coffee	12,818	8,146	4,391	25	17	201	38
13	Pan-vine	2	2	..	..	..	..	..
14	Rubber	44	29	15	..	..	..	..
15	Tea	270	146	124	..	..	..	..
16	Market gardeners, flower and fruit growers	22	18	1	1	..	2	..
	(*c*) Forestry	*309*	*250*	*1*	..	..	*58*	..
17	Forest officers, rangers, guards, etc. ..	141	119	..	..	..	22	..
18	Woodcutters and charcoal burners ..	168	131	1	..	..	36	..
	(*d*) Stock raising	*654*	*339*	*12*	*262*	*6*	*34*	*1*
21	Cattle and buffalo breeders and keepers ..	651	339	12	259	6	34	1
23	Herdsmen, shepherds and breeders of other animals	3	..	..	3	..	..	..
	Order 2.—*Fishing and hunting* ..	*51*	*27*	*5*	..	*17*	*2*	..
27	Fishing and pearling	51	27	5	..	17	2	..
	Class B.—Preparation and Supply of Material Substances	*11,170*	*7,337*	*943*	*104*	*26*	*2,591*	*169*
	SUB-CLASS III.—INDUSTRY ..	*4,991*	*3,180*	*628*	*40*	*19*	*984*	*140*
	Order 5.—*Textiles*	*75*	*61*	*9*	..	..	*4*	*1*
43	Cotton spinning, seizing and weaving ..	65	54	9	..	..	2	..
45	Rope, twine, string and other fibres ..	4	3	..	..	..	1	..
46	Wool carding, spinning and weaving ..	4	3	..	..	..	..	1
47	Silk spinning and weaving	2	1	..	..	..	1	..
	Order 6.—*Hides, skins and hard materials from the animal kingdom* ..	*2*	*2*	..	..	..	..	..
51	Working in leather	2	2	..	..	..	..	..

* *Groups for which returns are nil have been omitted.*

TABLE X

Occupation or Means of Livelihood—*cont.*

Group number.	Occupation.	Province. Total following occupation.	As principal occupation. Males.	As principal occupation. Females.	As working dependents. Males.	As working dependents. Females.	As subsidiary to other occupation. Males.	As subsidiary to other occupation. Females.
1	2	3	4	5	6	7	8	9
	Class B.—Preparation and Supply of Material Substances—*cont.*							
	SUB-CLASS III.—INDUSTRY—*cont.*							
	Order 7.—Wood	*1,166*	*679*	*149*	*5*	*2*	*211*	*120*
54	Sawyers	88	69	..	..	..	19	..
55	Carpenters, turners and joiners	452	387	..	5	..	60	..
56	Basket makers and other industries of woody materials including leaves, and thatchers and builders working with bamboo, reeds or similar materials ..	626	223	149	..	2	132	120
	Order 8.—Metals	*315*	*209*	*3*	*1*	..	*102*	..
58	Makers of arms, guns, etc.	2	..	..	..	..	2	..
59	Blacksmiths, other workers in iron, makers of implements	232	144	2	..	..	86	..
60	Workers in brass, copper and bell metal.	59	45	1	..	..	13	..
61	Workers in other metals (except precious metals)	22	20	..	1	..	1	..
	Order 9.—Ceramics	*331*	*131*	*119*	*2*	*9*	*68*	*2*
63	Potters and makers of earthenware ..	330	130	119	2	9	68	2
64	Brick and tile makers	1	1	..	..	..	..	..
	Order 10.—Chemical products properly so-called and analogous ..	*28*	*18*	..	*2*	..	*6*	*2*
67	Manufacture of aerated and mineral waters and ice	12	8	..	2	..	2	..
68	Manufacture and refining of vegetable oils	15	10	..	..	..	3	2
70	Others	1	..	..	..	..	1	..
	Order 11.—Food industries ..	*813*	*619*	*60*	*6*	..	*126*	*2*
71	Rice pounders and huskers and flour grinders	54	2	28	..	..	24	..
72	Grain-parchers, etc.	80	38	29	1	..	10	2
73	Butchers	43	41	2	..	..	..	..
76	Toddy-drawers	612	517	..	3	..	92	..
78	Manufacturers of tobacco	2	1	1	..	..	..	..
81	Others	22	20	..	2	..	..	..
	Order 12.—Industries of dress and the toilet.	*1,352*	*760*	*235*	*12*	*5*	*329*	*11*
82	Boot, shoe, sandal and clog makers ..	54	22	1	3	..	28	..
83	Tailors, milliners, dressmakers and darners	413	235	18	7	..	151	2
84	Embroiderers, hat-makers and makers of other articles of wear	2	1	..	..	..	1	..
85	Washing and cleaning	675	364	214	2	5	81	9
86	Barbers, hairdressers and wigmakers ..	208	138	2	..	..	68	..
	Order 14.—Building industries ..	*302*	*238*	*22*	..	..	*42*	..
90	Lime-burners, cement-workers; excavators and well-sinkers; stone-cutters and dressers; bricklayers and masons; builders (other than buildings made of bamboo or similar materials), painters, decorators of houses, tilers, plumbers, etc. ..	302	238	22	..	..	42	..
	Order 15.—Construction of means of transport	*75*	*66*	..	*8*	..	*1*	..
91	Persons engaged in making, assembling or repairing motor vehicles or cycles ..	6	6	..	..	..	..	..
92	Carriage, cart, palki, etc., makers and wheelwrights	69	60	..	8	..	1	..

TABLE X

Occupation or Means of Livelihood—*cont.*

Group number.	Occupation.	Province. Total following occupation.	As principal occupation. Males.	As principal occupation. Females.	As working dependents. Males.	As working dependents. Females.	As subsidiary to other occupation. Males.	As subsidiary to other occupation. Females.
1	2	3	4	5	6	7	8	9
	Class B.—Preparation and Supply of Material Substances—*cont.*							
	SUB-CLASS III.—INDUSTRY—*cont.*							
	Order 17.—Miscellaneous and undefined industries	*532*	*397*	*31*	*4*	*3*	*95*	*2*
95	Printers, engravers, bookbinders, etc. ..	6	5	..	..	..	1	..
97	Makers of clocks and surgical or scientific instruments, etc.	5	4	..	1	..	..	..
98	Makers of jewellery and ornaments ..	443	340	6	3	1	93	..
99	Other miscellaneous and undefined industries (toy-making, taxidermy, etc.) ..	1	1	..	..	..	..	..
100	Scavenging	77	47	25	..	2	1	2
	SUB-CLASS IV.—TRANSPORT ..	*2,438*	*1,502*	*11*	*26*	*2*	*892*	*5*
	Order 19.—Transport by water ..	*2*	*2*	..	..	..	..	..
102	Ship-owners, boat-owners and their employees, officers, mariners, etc., ship-brokers, boatmen and towmen ..	2	2	..	..	..	..	..
	Order 20.—Transport by road ..	*2,344*	*1,442*	*7*	*26*	*1*	*868*	..
105	Persons (other than labourers) employed on the construction and maintenance of roads and bridges	8	8	..	..	..	..	..
106	Labourers employed on roads and bridges.	258	218	1	1	1	37	..
107	Owners, managers and employees (excluding personal servants) connected with mechanically driven vehicles (including trams)	249	220	5	..	..	24	..
108	Owners, managers and employees (excluding personal servants) connected with other vehicles	1,767	949	..	25	..	793	..
110	Pack elephant, camel, mule, ass and bullock owners and drivers	1	1	..	..	..	..	..
111	Porters and messengers	61	46	1	..	..	14	..
	Order 21.—Transport by rail ..	*14*	*12*	..	..	..	*2*	..
112	Railway employees of all kinds other than coolies	14	12	..	..	..	2	..
	Order 22.—Post office, telegraph and telephone services	*78*	*46*	*4*	..	*1*	*22*	*5*
114	Post office, telegraph and telephone services	78	46	4	..	1	22	5
	SUB-CLASS V.—TRADE ..	*3,741*	*2,655*	*304*	*38*	*5*	*715*	*24*
	Order 23.—Banks, establishments of credit, exchange and insurance ..	*123*	*15*	*1*	..	..	*107*	..
115	Bank managers, moneylenders, exchange and insurance agents, money changers and brokers and their employees ..	123	15	1	..	..	107	..
	Order 24.—Brokerage, commission and export	*124*	*85*	*2*	*1*	..	*36*	..
116	Brokers, commission agents, commercial travellers, warehouse owners and employees	124	85	2	1	..	36	..
	Order 25.—Trade in textiles ..	*207*	*156*	*1*	*13*	..	*36*	*1*
117	Trade in piece-goods, wool, cotton, silk, hair and other textiles	207	156	1	13	..	36	1
	Order 26.—Trade in skins, leather and furs	*12*	*9*	..	..	..	*3*	..
118	Trade in skins, leather, furs, feathers, horn, etc., and the articles made from these	12	9	..	..	..	3	..

TABLE X

Occupation or Means of Livelihood—*cont.*

Group number.	Occupation.	Total following occupation.	Province. As principal occupation. Males.	Females.	As working dependents. Males.	Females.	As subsidiary to other occupation. Males.	Females.
1	2	3	4	5	6	7	8	9
	Class B.—Preparation and Supply of Material Substances—*cont.*							
	SUB-CLASS V.—TRADE—*cont.*							
	Order 27.—Trade in wood ..	***21***	***5***	***1***	..	..	***15***	..
119	Trade in wood (not firewood)	12	4	..	..	..	8	..
121	Trade in bamboos and canes	9	1	1	..	..	7	..
	Order 28.—Trade in metals ..	***43***	***32***	***1***	..	..	***10***	..
123	Trade in metals, machinery, knives, tools, etc.	43	32	1	..	..	10	..
	Order 30.—Trade in chemical products.	***4***	***4***	..	..	..	..	..
125	Drugs, dyes, paints, petroleum, explosives, etc.	4	4	..	..	..	..	..
	Order 31.—Hotels, cafes, restaurants, etc.	***342***	***272***	***29***	***4***	***1***	***35***	***1***
126	Vendors of wine, liquors, ærated waters and ice	108	86	2	..	..	20	..
127	Owners and managers of hotels, cook-shops, sarais, etc. (and employees) ..	190	161	10	4	1	14	..
128	Hawkers of drink and foodstuffs ..	44	25	17	..	..	1	1
	Order 32.—Other trade in foodstuffs ..	***2,133***	***1,548***	***199***	***17***	***3***	***358***	***8***
129	Grain and pulse dealers	315	222	25	..	..	66	2
130	Dealers in sweetmeats, sugar and spices ..	1,384	1,053	86	13	1	226	5
131	Dealers in dairy products, eggs and poultry.	87	49	28	1	1	8	..
134	Dealers in other foodstuffs	280	183	51	2	1	42	1
135	Dealers in tobacco	67	41	9	1	..	16	..
	Order 33.—Trade in clothing and toilet articles	***7***	***6***	..	..	..	***1***	..
138	Trade in ready-made clothing and other articles of dress and the toilet (hats, umbrellas, socks, ready-made shoes, perfumes, etc.)	7		..	..	..	1	..
	Order 34.—Trade in furniture ..	***30***	***15***	***4***	..	..	***11***	..
140	Hardware, cooking utensils, porcelain, crockery, glassware, bottles, articles for gardening, etc.	30	15	4	..	..	11	..
	Order 35.—Trade in building materials.	***4***	***1***	***1***	..	..	***2***	..
141	Trade in building materials (other than bricks, tiles and woody materials) ..	4	1	1	..	..	2	..
	Order 36.—Trade in means of transport.	***22***	***19***	..	..	..	***3***	..
142	Dealers and hirers in mechanical transport, motors, cycles, etc.	4	1	..	..	..	3	..
144	Dealers and hirers of elephants, camels, horses, cattle, asses, mules, etc. ..	18	18	..	..	..	..	..
	Order 37.—Trade in fuel ..	***1***	***1***	..	..	..	..	..
145	Dealers in firewood, charcoal, coal, cow-dung, etc.	1	1	..	..	..	..	..

TABLE X

Occupation or Means of Livelihood—*cont.*

Group number.	Occupation.	Province. Total following occupation.	As principal occupation. Males.	As principal occupation. Females.	As working dependents. Males.	As working dependents. Females.	As subsidiary to other occupation. Males.	As subsidiary to other occupation. Females.
1	2	3	4	5	6	7	8	9
	Class B.—Preparation and Supply of Material Substances—*cont.*							
	SUB-CLASS V.—TRADE —*cont.*							
	Order 38.—Trade in articles of luxury and those pertaining to letters and the arts and sciences ..	***123***	***65***	***28***	***1***	***1***	***21***	***7***
146	Dealers in precious stones, jewellery (real and imitation), clocks, optical instruments, etc.	5	5	..	..	..	..	..
147	Dealers in common bangles, bead necklaces, fans, small articles, toys, hunting and fishing tackle, flowers, etc.	84	31	25	1	1	19	7
148	Publishers, booksellers, stationers, dealers in music, pictures, musical instruments and curiosities	34	29	3	..	..	2	..
	Order 39.—Trade of other sorts ..	***545***	***422***	***37***	***2***	..	***77***	***7***
150	General storekeepers and shopkeepers otherwise unspecified	537	416	37	2	..	75	7
152	Other trades (including farmers of pounds, tools and markets)	8	6	..	..	..	2	..
	Class C.—Public Administration and Liberal Arts	***2,105***	***1,350***	***100***	***10***	***3***	***640***	***2***
	SUB-CLASS VI.—PUBLIC FORCE ..	***198***	***180***	..	..	..	***18***	..
	Order 40.—Army	***2***	***2***	..	..	..	..	..
153	Army (Imperial)	2	2	..	..	..	..	..
	Order 43.—Police	***196***	***178***	..	..	..	***18***	..
157	Police	196	178	..	..	..	18	..
	SUB-CLASS VII.—PUBLIC ADMINISTRATION.	***660***	***350***	***3***	***1***	..	***306***	..
	Order 44.—Public Administration ..	***660***	***350***	***3***	***1***	..	***306***	..
159	Service of the State	366	285	2	1	..	78	..
161	Municipal and other local (not village) service	36	30	1	..	..	5	..
162	Village officials and servants other than watchmen	258	35	..	..	..	223	..
	SUB-CLASS VIII.—PROFESSIONS AND LIBERAL ARTS.	***1,247***	***820***	***97***	***9***	***3***	***316***	***2***
	Order 45.—Religion	***448***	***293***	***16***	***8***	***3***	***127***	***1***
163	Priests, ministers, etc.	61	41	..	2	..	18	..
164	Monks, nuns, religious mendicants ..	3	2	..	1	..	..	..
165	Other religious workers	4	2	..	..	1	1	..
166	Servants in religious edifices, burial and burning grounds, pilgrim conductors, circumcisers, etc.	380	248	16	5	2	108	1
	Order 46.—Law	***33***	***27***	..	..	..	***6***	..
167	Lawyers of all kinds, including qazis, law agents and mukhtiars	18	18	..	..	..	..	..
168	Lawyers' clerks, petition-writers, etc. ..	15	9	..	..	..	6	..
	Order 47.—Medicine	***167***	***129***	***22***	..	..	***16***	..
169	Registered medical practitioners including oculists	21	19	..	..	..	2	..
170	Other persons practising the healing arts without being registered	84	69	5	..	..	10	..
172	Midwives, vaccinators, compounders, nurses, masseurs, etc.	60	39	17	..	..	4	..
173	Veterinary surgeons	2	2	..	..	..	..	..

TABLE X

Occupation or Means of Livelihood—*cont.*

Group number.	Occupation.	Province. Total following occupation.	As principal occupation. Males.	As principal occupation. Females.	As working dependents. Males.	As working dependents. Females.	As subsidiary to other occupation. Males.	As subsidiary to other occupation. Females.
1	2	3	4	5	6	7	8	9
	Class C.—Public Administration and Liberal Arts—*cont.*							
	SUB-CLASS VIII.—PROFESSIONS AND LIBERAL ARTS—*cont.*							
	Order 48.—Instruction ..	*409*	*296*	*44*	*1*	..	*67*	*1*
174	Professors and teachers of all kinds ..	405	292	44	1	..	67	1
175	Clerks and servants connected with education	4	4	..	..	..	..	..
	Order 49.—Letters, arts and sciences (other than 44)	*190*	*75*	*15*	..	..	*100*	..
177	Architects, surveyors, engineers and their employees (not being State servants).	2	2	..	..	..	..	..
178	Authors, editors, journalists and photographers	4	3	..	..	..	1	..
181	Horoscope casters, astrologers, fortune-tellers, wizards, witches and mediums.	40	20	1	..	..	19	..
182	Musicians (composers and performers other than military), actors, dancers, etc. ..	137	46	14	..	..	77	..
183	Managers and employees of places of public entertainments, race courses, societies, clubs	1	1	..	..	..	..	..
184	Conjurors, acrobats, reciters, exhibitors of curiosities and wild animals, etc. ..	6	3	..	..	..	3	..
	Class D.—Miscellaneous	***49,322***	***9,264***	***5,429***	***1,152***	***25,139***	***634***	***7,704***
	SUB-CLASS IX.—PERSONS LIVING ON THEIR INCOME	*103*	*33*	*4*	*1*	..	*65*	..
	Order 50.—Persons living principally on their income	*103*	*33*	*4*	*1*	..	*65*	
185	Proprietors (other than of agricultural land), fund and scholarship holders and pensioners	103	33	4	1	..	65	
	SUB-CLASS X.—DOMESTIC SERVICE ..	*35,733*	*1,104*	*541*	*1,054*	*25,024*	*313*	*7,697*
	Order 51.—Domestic service ..	*35,733*	*1,104*	*541*	*1,054*	*25,024*	*313*	*7,697*
186	Private motor-drivers and cleaners ..	16	14	..	..	..	2	..
187	Other domestic service	35,717	1,090	541	1,054	25,024	311	7,697
	SUB-CLASS XI.—INSUFFICIENTLY DESCRIBED OCCUPATIONS ..	*13,273*	*7,983*	*4,832*	*94*	*113*	*246*	*5*
	Order 52.—General terms which do not indicate a definite occupation ..	*13,273*	*7,983*	*4,832*	*94*	*113*	*246*	*5*
188	Manufacturers, businessmen and contractors otherwise unspecified	152	124	..	3	..	25	..
189	Cashiers, accountants, book-keepers, clerks and other employees in unspecified offices and warehouses and shops ..	514	408	2	10	..	94	..
190	Mechanics otherwise unspecified	8	8	..	..	..	..	..
191	Labourers and workmen otherwise unspecified	12,599	7,443	4,830	81	113	127	5
	SUB-CLASS XII.—UNPRODUCTIVE ..	*213*	*144*	*52*	*3*	*2*	*10*	*2*
	Order 54.—Beggars, vagrants, prostitutes.	*213*	*144*	*52*	*3*	*2*	*10*	*2*
193	Beggars and vagrants	213	144	52	3	2	10	2

TABLE XIII

Literacy by Religion and Age.

Religion.	Age.	Population. Total. Persons.	Total. Males.	Total. Females.	Literate. Persons.	Literate. Males.	Literate. Females.	Illiterate. Persons.	Illiterate. Males.	Illiterate. Females.	Literate in English. Persons.	Literate in English. Males.	Literate in English. Females.
1	2	3	4	5	6	7	8	9	10	11	12	13	14
All religions.	Total ..	*163,327*	*90,575*	*72,752*	*25,336*	*19,892*	*5,444*	*137,991*	*70,683*	*67,308*	*3,982*	*3,279*	*703*
	0-5 ..	19,532	9,668	9,854	..	..	..	19,522	9,668	9,854	..	..	..
	5-10 ..	18,616	9,527	9,089	1,531	1,025	506	17,085	8,502	8,583	159	99	60
	10-15 ..	18,954	9,993	8,961	2,622	1,777	845	16,332	8,216	8,116	387	266	121
	15-20 ..	16,639	9,129	7,510	3,527	2,499	1,028	13,112	6,630	6,482	688	524	164
	20 and over.	89,596	52,258	37,838	17,656	14,591	3,065	71,940	37,667	34,273	2,748	2,390	358
Hindu ..	Total ..	*146,007*	*79,559*	*66,448*	*22,418*	*17,395*	*5,023*	*123,589*	*62,164*	*61,425*	*3,393*	*2,800*	*593*
	0-5 ..	17,914	8,835	9,079	..	..	..	17,914	8,835	9,079	..	..	..
	5-10 ..	17,040	8,672	8,368	1,405	940	465	15,635	7,732	7,903	143	87	56
	10-15 ..	17,159	8,949	8,210	2,416	1,626	790	14,743	7,323	7,420	356	245	111
	15-20 ..	14,655	7,845	6,810	3,180	2,210	970	11,475	5,635	5,840	615	468	147
	20 and over.	79,239 *	45,258 *	33,981	15,417	12,619 *	2,798	63,822	32,639	31,183	2,279	2,000 *	279
Muslim ..	Total ..	*13,777*	*8,943*	*4,834*	*1,819*	*1,686*	*133*	*11,958*	*7,257*	*4,701*	*117*	*116*	*1*
	0-5 ..	1,222	621	601	..	..	..	1,222	621	601	..	..	..
	5-10 ..	1,226	671	555	57	43	14	1,169	628	541	3	3	..
	10-15 ..	1,424	842	582	107	89	18	1,317	753	564	6	6	..
	15-20 ..	1,621	1,074	547	226	204	22	1,395	870	525	18	18	..
	20 and over	8,284	5,735	2,549	1,429	1,350	79	6,855	4,385	2,470	90	89	1
Christian.	Total ..	*3,430* †	*2,015*	*1,415*	*1,051*	*783*	*268*	*2,379*	*1,232*	*1,147*	*456*	*353*	*103*
	0-5 ..	369	203	166	..	..	..	369	203	166	..	..	..
	5-10 ..	337	179	158	62	39	23	275	140	135	11	8	3
	10-15 ..	357	196	161	93	60	33	264	136	128	23	14	9
	15-20 ..	351	205	146	115	83	32	236	122	114	53	37	16
	20 and over.	2,016	1,232	784	781	601	180	1,235	631	604	369	294	75
Jain ..	Total ..	*83*	*43*	*40*	*32*	*21*	*11*	*51*	*22*	*29*	*3*	*3*	..
	0-5 ..	14	8	6	..	..	..	14	8	6	..	..	..
	5-10 ..	9	3	6	4	2	2	5	1	4	..	..	..
	10-15 ..	11	5	6	5	2	3	6	3	3	1	1	..
	15-20 ..	10	4	6	5	2	3	5	2	3	1	1	..
	20 and over.	39	23	16	18	15	3	21	8	13	1	1	..
Zoroastrian (Parsi).	Total ..	*27*	*12*	*15*	*16*	*7*	*9*	*11*	*5*	*6*	*13*	*7*	*6*
	0-5 ..	3	1	2	..	..	..	3	1	2	..	..	..
	5-10	4	2	2	3	1	2	1	1	..	2	1	1
	10-15 ..	3	1	2	1	..	1	2	1	1	1	..	1
	15-20 ..	2	1	1	1	..	1	1	1	..	1	..	1
	20 and over.	15	7	8	11	6	5	4	1	3	9	6	3
Buddhist.	Total ..	*3*	*3*	..	..	..	..	*3*	*3*	..	..	..	..
	0-5 ..	..	..	..	..	..	..	..	..	..	..	..	..
	5-10 ..	..	..	..	..	..	..	..	..	..	..	..	..
	10-15 ..	..	..	..	..	..	..	..	..	..	..	..	..
	15-20 ..	..	..	..	..	..	..	..	..	..	..	..	..
	20 and over.	3	3	..	..	..	..	3	3	..	..	..	..

* Includes one Brahmo male.

† Five persons (three males and two females), returned under 'Indefinite Beliefs' in Table XVI have been classed as Christians for the purpose of this table.

TABLE XIV

Literacy by Selected Communities.

Race, Tribe or Caste.	Population (7 Years and Over). Total. Persons.	Males.	Females.	Literate. Persons.	Males.	Females.	Illiterate. Persons.	Males.	Females.	Literate in English (7 Years and Over). Persons.	Males.	Females.
1	2	3	4	5	6	7	8	9	10	11	12	13
Adi-Dravida (D.C.)	42	21	21	..	..	..	42	21	21	..	..	..
Adiya (D.C.)	4	4	..	..	..	..	4	4	..	..	..	..
Amma Kodaga	547	281	266	259	198	61	288	83	205	40	36	4
Anglo-Indian	77	40	37	56	26	30	21	14	7	56	26	30
Arya Vaisya (Komati)	170	85	85	74	57	17	96	28	68	11	9	2
Balagai (D.C.)	114	64	50	..	..	..	114	64	50	..	..	..
Bant	1,209	803	406	233	204	29	976	599	377	44	43	1
Boya	375	196	179	7	7	..	368	189	179	..	..	..
Brahman—Kanarese	1,085	602	483	662	497	165	423	105	318	212	190	22
Brahman—Malayalam	21	13	8	11	9	2	10	4	6	1	1	..
Brahman—Tamil	88	42	46	64	38	26	24	4	20	28	22	6
Brahman—Telugu	9	8	1	7	6	1	2	2	..	5	5	..
Gauda	11,579	6,213	5,366	2,115	1,877	238	9,464	4,336	5,128	158	154	4
Golla	437	245	192	65	59	6	372	186	186	2	2	..
Holeya (D.C.)	274	161	113	2	2	..	272	159	113	1	1	..
Kalloda (D.C.)	2	2	..	..	..	..	2	2	..	..	..	..
Kodaga	33,753	17,071	16,682	13,184	9,381	3,803	20,569	7,690	12,879	2,400	1,892	508
Korama (D.C.)	106	57	49	10	10	..	96	47	49	1	1	..
Kudiya (D.C.)	436	218	218	..	..	..	436	218	218	..	..	..
Kuruba	5,633	3,071	2,562	27	23	4	5,606	3,048	2,558	1	1	..
Labbai	189	111	78	50	41	9	139	70	69	1	1	..
Lingayat	4,400	1,968	2,432	725	650	75	3,675	1,318	2,357	102	82	20
Lippara (D.C.)	2	2	..	..	..	..	2	2	..	..	..	..
Madiga (D.C.)	179	97	82	81	43	38	98	54	44	..	..	..
Maleya (D.C.)	100	58	42	24	23	1	76	35	41	..	..	..
Mappilla	7,906	5,587	2,319	1,019	960	59	6,887	4,627	2,260	27	20	7
Maratha	520	352	168	51	38	13	469	314	155	7	7	..
Medara (D.C.)	33	29	4	..	..	..	33	29	4	..	..	..
Muchi (D.C.)	16	7	9	..	..	..	16	7	9	..	..	..
Mundala (D.C.)	79	47	32	2	1	1	77	46	31	..	..	..
Nale Kanavaru (D.C.)	9	9	..	..	..	..	9	9	..	..	..	..
Nayar	1,222	1,076	146	281	273	8	941	803	138	15	13	2
Pale (D.C.)	2,902	1,995	907	8	8	..	2,894	1,987	907	..	..	..
Panchama (D.C.)	17,011	9,726	7,285	192	188	4	16,819	9,538	7,281	5	5	..
Panikkar (D.C.)	4	1	3	1	1	..	3	..	3	..	..	..
Paraiyan (D.C.)	290	162	128	5	4	1	285	158	127	..	..	..
Samagara (D.C.)	5	4	1	..	..	..	5	4	1	..	..	..
Surava (D.C.)	3	3	..	..	..	..	3	3	..	..	..	..
Telaga	234	122	112	37	32	5	197	90	107	..	..	..
Vakkaliga	6,875	3,711	3,164	591	547	44	6,284	3,164	3,120	22	21	1
Viswa Brahman—Tamil	85	48	37	15	15	..	70	33	37	..	..	..
Viswa Brahman—Telugu	18	10	8	3	3	..	15	7	8	..	..	..
Yadava	4	4	..	1	1	..	3	3	..	..	..	..
Yerava	10,365	5,539	4,826	23	15	8	10,342	5,524	4,818	4	..	4

D.C. = Depressed classes.

TABLE XV (Part I).

Mother-tongue.

Mother-tongue. 1	Persons. 2	Males. 3	Females. 4
TOTAL ..	*163,327*	*90,575*	*72,752*
A.—VERNACULARS OF INDIA	*162,998*	*90,393*	*72,605*
(i) *Vernaculars of the Province*	*54,611*	*27,895*	*26,716*
Kodagu or Coorgi	44,585	22,667	21,918
Yerava	10,026	5,228	4,798
(ii) *Vernaculars foreign to the Province*	*108,387*	*62,498*	*45,889*
Gujarati	53	33	20
Hindōstāni	4,378	2,402	1,976
Kanarese	62,769	33,066	29,703
Konkani	2,331	1,368	963
Korava	6	4	2
Kurumba	2,394	1,244	1,150
Lambādi	7	7	..
Malayalam	14,914	11,260	3,654
Marathi	1,577	871	706
Tamil	3,007	1,752	1,255
Telugu	2,668	1,450	1,218
Tulu	14,275	9,034	5,241
Hindi	4	3	1
Punjabi	4	4	..
B.—VERNACULARS OF OTHER ASIATIC COUNTRIES	*19*	*11*	*8*
Arabic	19	11	8
C.—EUROPEAN LANGUAGES	*310*	*171*	*139*
English	254	146	108
French	5	1	4
Irish	1	1	..
Portuguese	50	23	27

TABLE XV (Part II).

Subsidiary Language.

Mother-tongue.	Returned by			Subsidiary language. Kodagu or Coorgi.			Yerava.			Malayalam.			Kanarese.			Tulu.		
	Persons.	Males.	Females.	Persons.	Males.	Females.	Persons.	Males.	Females.	Persons.	Males.	Females.	Persons.	Males.	Females.	Persons.	Males.	Females.
1	2	3	4	5	6	7	8	9	10	11	12	13	14	15	16	17	18	19
Kodagu or Coorgi.	44,585	22,667	21,918	..	..	..	1	..	1	58	43	15	22,870	13,216	9,654	19	14	5
Yerava	10,026	5,228	4,798	322	180	142	..	..	..	6	6	..	1,077	589	488	..	..	..
Malayalam	14,914	11,260	3,654	285	192	93	..	..	..	..	..	..	2,037	1,679	358	168	141	27
Kanarese	62,769	33,066	29,703	1,342	795	547	1	..	1	48	36	12	..	..	..	801	473	328
Tulu	14,275	9,034	5,241	443	279	164	10	5	5	126	93	33	5,433	3,589	1,844	..	..	..

TABLE XVI (Part I).

Religion.

Province.	Population.			Hindu.			Muslim.		
	Persons.	Males.	Females.	Persons.	Males.	Females.	Persons.	Males.	Females.
1	2	3	4	5	6	7	8	9	10
Coorg	163,327	90,575	72,752	146,007	79,559	66,448	13,777	8,943	4,834

Province.	Christian.			Tribal.			Jain.			Buddhist.			Zoroastrian (Parsi).			Others. (Agnostic).		
	Persons.	Males.	Females.	Persons.	Males.	Females.	Persons.	Males.	Females.	Persons.	Males.	Females.	Persons.	Males.	Females.	Persons.	Males.	Females.
	11	12	13	14	15	16	17	18	19	20	21	22	23	24	25	26	27	28
Coorg	3,425	2,012	1,413	..	..	..	83	43	40	3	3	..	27	12	15	5	3	2

TABLE XVI (Part II).

Hindu and Christian Details.

Province.	Hindu.											
	Total.			Brahmanic.			Arya.			Brahmo.		
	Persons.	Males.	Females.	Persons.	Males.	Females.	Persons.	Males.	Females.	Persons.	Males.	Females.
1	2	3	4	5	6	7	8	9	10	11	12	13
Coorg	146,007	79,559	66,448	146,006	79,558	66,448	..	..	..	1	1	..

Province.	Christian.														
	Total.			Roman Catholics.			Syrians.						Others.		
							Romo Syrians.			Other Syrians.					
	Persons.	Males.	Females.	Persons.	Males.	Females.	Persons.	Males.	Females.	Persons.	Males.	Females.	Persons.	Males.	Females.
	14	15	16	17	18	19	20	21	22	23	24	25	26	27	28
Coorg	3,425	2,012	1,413	2,808	1,686	1,122	..	..	..	16	14	2	601	312	289

TABLE XVII

Race, Tribe or Caste

Race, tribe or caste.	Total. Persons.	Males.	Females.
1	2	3	4
Adi-Dravida (D.C.)	52	23	29
Adiya (D.C.)	5	5	..
Agasa	1,397	786	611
Amma Kodaga	666	336	330
Anglo-Indian	84	44	40
Arya Vaisya (Komati)	211	100	111
Balagai (D.C.)	130	72	58
Bant	1,369	872	497
Boya	443	226	217
Brahman—Kanarese	1,258	685	573
Brahman—Malayalam	24	14	10
Brahman—Tamil	115	53	62
Brahman—Telugu	10	8	2
Ganiga	286	164	122
Gauda	14,016	7,388	6,628
Golla	520	289	231
Holeya (D.C.)	320	185	135
Kalloda (D.C.)	2	2	..
Kodaga	41,026	20,752	20,274
Korama (D.C.)	128	63	65
Kudiya (D.C.) (P.T.)	549	270	279
Kuruba	6,867	3,710	3,157
Labbai	218	126	92
Lingayat	5,068	2,250	2,818
Lippara (D.C.)	4	3	1
Madiga (D.C.)	217	122	95
Maleya (D.C.)	123	71	52
Mappilla	8,804	6,051	2,753
Maratha (P.T.)	540	360	180
Medara (D.C.)	41	37	4
Muchi (D.C.)	20	9	11
Mundala (D.C.)	87	52	35
Nale Kanavaru (D.C.)	9	9	..
Nayar	1,278	1,100	178
Pale (D.C.)	3,192	2,128	1,064
Panchama (D.C.)	19,571	10,971	8,600
Panikkar (D.C.)	5	2	3
Paraiyan (D.C.)	340	184	156
Rajput	97	58	39
Samagara (D.C.)	5	4	1
Surava (D.C.)	3	3	..
Telaga	280	142	138
Vakkaliga	7,948	4,233	3,715
Visvabrahman—Tamil	104	58	46
Visvabrahman—Telugu	24	13	11
Yadava	5	5	..
Yerava	12,810	6,763	6,047

D.C. = Depressed Classes. P.T. = Primitive Tribes.

TABLE XVIII

Variation of Population of Selected Tribes.

Tribe and locality.	Persons. 1931	1921	1911	1901	1891	1881	Variation. 1921 to 1931	1911 to 1921	1901 to 1911	1891 to 1901	1881 to 1891	Net variation, 1881 to 1931.
1	2	3	4	5	6	7	8	9	10	11	12	13
Kudiya	549	414	541	589	642	..	+ 135	— 127	— 48	— 53	..	..
North Coorg	375	..	..	..	..	..	..	..	..	..	..	..
South Coorg	174	..	..	..	..	..	..	..	..	..	..	..
Maratha	540	1,710	1,476	2,457	2,384	..	— 1,170	+ 234	— 981	+ 73	..	..
North Coorg	446	..	..	..	..	..	..	..	..	..	..	..
South Coorg	94	..	..	..	..	..	..	..	..	..	..	..

Tribe and locality.	Males. 1931	1921	1911	1901	1891	1881	Females. 1931	1921	1911	1901	1891	1881
	14	15	16	17	18	19	20	21	22	23	24	25
Kudiya	270	205	258	284	321	..	279	209	283	305	321	..
North Coorg	189	..	..	..	..	..	186	..	..	..	..	..
South Coorg	81	..	..	..	..	..	93	..	..	..	..	..
Maratha	860	1,101	1,438	1,431	1,388	..	180	609	38	1,026	996	..
North Coorg	309	..	..	..	..	..	137	..	..	..	..	..
South Coorg	51	..	..	..	..	..	43	..	..	..	..	..

TABLE XIX

European and Allied Races and Anglo-Indians by Race and Age.

Province.	Total.			A.—European and Allied Races. (a) British Subjects. All ages.			0–13		14–16		17–23		24–33		34–43	
	Persons.	Males.	Females.	Persons.	Males.	Females.	Males.	Females.	Males.	Females.	Males.	Females.	Males.	Females.	Males.	Females.
1	2	3	4	5	6	7	8	9	10	11	12	13	14	15	16	17
Coorg	138	73	65	122	69	53	11	9	..	..	4	6	15	14	18	9

Province.	A.—European and Allied Races—cont. (a) British Subjects. 44–53		54 and over.		(b) Others. All ages.			0–13		14–16		17–23		24–33		34–43	
	Males.	Females.	Males.	Females.	Persons.	Males.	Females.	Males.	Females.	Males.	Females.	Males.	Females.	Males.	Females.	Males.	Females.
	18	19	20	21	22	23	24	25	26	27	28	29	30	31	32	33	34
Coorg	7	7	14	8	16	4	12	..	5	..	..	..	..	3	2	1	1

Province.	A.—Europeans and Allied Races—cont. (b) Others. 44–53		54 and over.		B.—Anglo-Indians. All ages.			0–3		4–6		7–13		14–16	
	Males.	Females.	Males.	Females.	Persons.	Males.	Females.	Males.	Females.	Males.	Females.	Males.	Females.	Males.	Females.
	35	36	37	38	39	40	41	42	43	44	45	46	47	48	49
Coorg	..	1	..	3	84	44	40	2	2	2	1	2	7	2	2

Province.	B.—Anglo-Indians—cont. 17–19		20–29		30–39		40–49		50–59		60–69		70 and over.	
	Males.	Females.	Males.	Females.	Males.	Females.	Males.	Females.	Males.	Females.	Males.	Females.	Males.	Females.
	50	51	52	53	54	55	56	57	58	59	60	61	62	63
Coorg	5	4	10	8	5	7	7	4	5	3	3	1	1	1

PROVINCIAL TABLES

PROVINCIAL TABLE I

Area and Population of Taluks.

Name of the taluk.	Area in square miles.	Number of Towns.	Number of Villages.	Number of occupied houses.	Population 1931 Persons.	Population 1931 Males.	Population 1931 Females.	Population 1921 (both sexes).	Percentage variation 1921 to 1931.	Percentage variation 1911 to 1921.	Number of persons per square mile in 1931.
	2	3	4	5	6	7	8	9	10	11	12
Coorg	***1,593***	***2***	***378***	***33,906***	***163,327***	***90,575***	***72,752***	***163,838***	***— 0·3***	***— 6·4***	***103***
North Coorg	760	1	232	17,050	78,747	43,486	35,261	76,539	+ 2·9	— 6·2	104
South Coorg	833	1	146	16,856	84,580	47,089	37,491	87,299	— 3·1	— 6·5	102

PROVINCIAL TABLE II

Population of Districts and Taluks by Religion and Literacy.

District and taluk.	Hindus. Brahmans. Number of persons. Males.	Females.	Brahmans. Number literate. Males.	Females.	Other Hindus. Number of persons. Males.	Females.	Other Hindus. Number literate. Males.	Females.	Depressed Classes. Number of persons. Males.	Females.	Depressed Classes. Number literate. Males.	Females.
	2	3	4	5	6	7	8	9	10	11	12	13
Coorg	***1,472***	***1,251***	***980***	***326***	***63,512***	***54,429***	***16,097***	***4,639***	***14,575***	***10,768***	***318***	***58***
North Coorg	826	713	577	205	29,145	25,335	6,703	1,438	8,927	6,615	182	45
South Coorg	646	538	403	121	34,367	29,094	9,394	3,201	5,648	4,153	136	13

District and taluk.	Jains. Number of persons. Males.	Females.	Jains. Number literate. Males.	Females.	Sikhs. Number of persons. Males.	Females.	Sikhs. Number literate. Males.	Females.	Muslims. Number of persons. Males.	Females.	Muslims. Number literate. Males.	Females.	Christians. Number of persons. Males.	Females.	Christians. Number literate. Males.	Females.
	14	15	16	17	18	19	20	21	22	23	24	25	26	27	28	29
Coorg	***43***	***40***	***21***	***11***	..	..	..	..	***8,943***	***4,834***	***1,686***	***133***	***†2,015***	***†1,415***	***783***	***268***
North Coorg	15	6	5	..	..	..	..	..	3,557	1,914	664	61	1,007	669	386	173
South Coorg	28	34	16	11	..	..	..	..	5,386	2,920	1,022	72	1,008	746	397	95

District and taluk.	Tribal. Number of persons. Males.	Females.	Tribal. Number literate. Males.	Females.	Others. Number of persons. Males.	Females.	Others. Number literate. Males.	Females.	Number Literate. Age 0–15. Males.	Females.	Number Literate. Age 15–20. Males.	Females.	Number Literate. Age 20 and over. Males.	Females.	Literate in English. Males.	Females.
	30	31	32	33	34	35	36	37	38	39	40	41	42	43	44	45
Coorg	..	..	..	..	***15***	***15***	***7***	***9***	***2,802***	***1,351***	***2,499***	***1,028***	***14,591***	***3,065***	***3,279***	***703***
North Coorg	..	..	..	..	9	9	6	8	1,128	490	1,079	367	6,316	1,073	1,541	436
South Coorg	..	..	..	..	6	6	1	1	1,674	861	1,420	661	8,275	1,992	1,738	267

† Includes Agnostic M. 3 F2.

PROVINCIAL TABLE III

Population of Taluks, Municipalities and Towns by Age and Sex.

Taluks, Municipalities or Towns.	Population. Persons.	Population. Males.	Population. Females.	0–1. Males.	0–1. Females.	1–5. Males.	1–5. Females.	5–10. Males.	5–10. Females.	10–15. Males.	10–15. Females.
	2	3	4	5	6	7	8	9	10	11	12
Coorg	***163,327***	***90,575***	***72,752***	***2,127***	***2,186***	***7,541***	***7,668***	***9,527***	***9,089***	***9,993***	***8,961***
Taluks—											
North Coorg	**78,747**	43,486	35,261	1,001	1,085	3,393	3,609	4,431	4,431	4,837	4,458
South Coorg	**84,580**	47,089	37,491	1,126	1,101	4,148	4,059	5,096	4,658	5,156	4,503
Municipalities—											
Mercara	**5,995**	3,427	2,568	64	73	260	249	383	366	385	375
Virarajendrapet ..	**3,832**	2,421	1,411	42	30	136	151	197	148	251	154

Taluks, Municipalities or Towns.	15–20. Males.	15–20. Females.	20–30. Males.	20–30. Females.	30–40. Males.	30–40. Females.	40–50. Males.	40–50. Females.	50–60. Males.	50–60. Females.	60 and over. Males.	60 and over. Females.
	13	14	15	16	17	18	19	20	21	22	23	24
Coorg	***9,129***	***7,510***	***19,619***	***15,239***	***16,339***	***10,312***	***9,378***	***5,924***	***4,418***	***3,446***	***2,504***	***2,417***
Taluks—												
North Coorg	4,604	3,710	9,830	7,481	7,973	4,984	4,373	2,796	1,914	1,574	1,130	1,133
South Coorg	4,525	3,800	9,789	7,758	8,366	5,328	5.005	3,128	2,504	1,872	1,374	1,284
Municipalities—												
Mercara	396	255	737	469	539	312	353	221	181	136	129	112
Virarajendrapet ..	299	161	636	290	438	216	232	127	122	80	68	54